LETTERS ON EDUCATION

LETTERS

ON

EDUCATION

BY

EDWARD LYTTELTON,
M.A., D.D., D.C.L.

AUTHOR OF *MOTHERS AND SONS*

What manner of child shall this be?

CAMBRIDGE
AT THE UNIVERSITY PRESS
1922

CAMBRIDGE
UNIVERSITY PRESS

University Printing House, Cambridge CB2 8BS, United Kingdom

Cambridge University Press is part of the University of Cambridge.

It furthers the University's mission by disseminating knowledge in the pursuit of education, learning and research at the highest international levels of excellence.

www.cambridge.org
Information on this title: www.cambridge.org/9781107536968

© Cambridge University Press 1922

This publication is in copyright. Subject to statutory exception and to the provisions of relevant collective licensing agreements, no reproduction of any part may take place without the written permission of Cambridge University Press.

First published 1922
First paperback edition 2015

A catalogue record for this publication is available from the British Library

ISBN 978-1-107-53696-8 Paperback

Cambridge University Press has no responsibility for the persistence or accuracy of URLs for external or third-party internet websites referred to in this publication, and does not guarantee that any content on such websites is, or will remain, accurate or appropriate.

PREFACE

IN times like the present no one with a scrap of civic conscience can publish a book without a qualm. We are told by all sorts of high·authorities that now, more than ever, all our labour ought to be productive, really useful, needed. But a book means much labour, and supposing after all it is superfluous, what then?

In truth, there is only one justification for such a perilous venture. It is that the world in its anxiety is asking for the Gospel of brotherhood. A few years ago a writer with a social message to deliver would have had to apologize unless he disguised its Christian tone. To-day there is less need to do so. The Church in short is given an opportunity of witnessing to and exhibiting the "mind of Christ."

But a new peril confronts us. The world clamours for the Gospel that the fabric of society may be saved. That object is urged on us as if it were a plain truism that the saving of the social order must be the motive of Christian service. Yet this is a delusion. Christ never said "Mend the world," but He did say "Teach it"; and the results of the teaching He did not disclose. We are called upon to show the spirit of Christ. But that is impossible if we aim at anything but what He enjoined. He commanded us to teach, not because the teaching would save society, but because it would be unpalatable; because the Truth is the Truth: majestic, sublime, austere and lifegiving : and the one duty committed to every member of the Church is to testify to the Gospel message and leave the result in God's hand.

The signs of the times show plainly that we have got wrong in our interpretation of life; wrong, that is, as to the question "Why are we in the world?" Each nation has been blindly striving to make the world pleasant as a place of habitation. The purpose has been wrong and the means adopted for attaining it have been futile. The world is now calling on the Church to keep the original object in view still, but to devise a more successful method of attaining it. The demand is absurd. If we teach the truth with the object of making ourselves comfortable, we turn it into a lie, and the outcome will be fresh horrors, havoc and ruin.

Nevertheless the world is right in yearning for a "new spirit": that is why we must be concerned with the children. So not as a step in Reconstruction—a clumsy, impious word—but as an invitation to simple obedience I submit the following suggestions for the home-training of the young.

Hoping that many parents will read them, and aware of the danger of dullness, I have compressed the principles into an Introduction, but expanded them in the form of letters. The later batch of letters illustrate some practical applications of the principles.

I earnestly trust that if to any readers the main propositions seem disputable, they will put it down to the clumsiness of my statement, not to any falseness in the message.

E. L.

June 1921

INTRODUCTION

NO perplexity at the present time is so baffling as that which prevails far and wide on the subject of education. It seems that the more we write and talk, the more experiments we make, the more money we pay, the less we know. It is moreover peculiarly harassing that, just when trainers of the young are distracted by noisy and barren controversy or immersed in a dispiriting routine of work, the world at large is clamouring to them to turn out a generation of young people with sounder notions about life than the last, and to do this as soon as possible, for there is an ugly abyss yawning in front of us all towards which we continue to slide. Discord, meantime, reigns far and wide, and such unanimity as exists is of the sort which impelled the Gadarene swine full speed down the hill-side to be drowned in the sea.

Yet there can be no serious doubt that our bewilder-ment takes its rise from a kind of double-mindedness which the British race is specially prone to favour, while being wholly unaware of what is going on. The large majority of educators are striving to achieve a certain temporal success which would, they think, make this world a more comfortable place to live in. In pursuit of this aim they talk much about character-training: not their own characters but those of the children. The others, a small minority, are not concerned with any question of success or of temporal result whatever; but only with the principles of life, and conduct which are given us in the New Testament. They concentrate on training the Christ-like character, irrespective of what the result would be, but confident that it will be far more glorious than any of us either desire or deserve. They are able to see that the wreckage of life and loss of peace by which we are dismayed in the world to-day are due to our efforts to mend the world directly: and that the only hope of mending it lies in forgetting it: or rather in using it as a stepping-stone to a higher life. That is to deal with the world *indirectly*: by so grappling with the problems of earth as to infuse into them the life that is in Heaven: by regarding the anxieties of time as warnings to turn our minds to eternity: yet not to ignore the human, but to uplift it by admitting into it the divine.

At first that programme seems to promise agreement, and to be, in short, merely the right way of being practically efficient. Religion, as many worldlings admit, is an indispensable aid to their worldly endeavours. Earth is doomed unless we transform it by the contact of Heaven; man has to mend this life, and can only do so by calling on God to help him. True, so far: but the cart is before the horse all the time. God is the end, not man: and to strive towards Him as the end is a wholly different thing from using Him as a means. Far better ignore Him altogether: for He is either everything or nothing. To aim at securing our own happiness along with the doing of God's will is to put God and man on an equality: that is tantamount to putting man first and God nowhere. Dimly conscious of this deadly disease of mind, and ascribing the symptoms to self-regard or ego-centricity, men have preached Altruism, meaning the working for the happiness of others in forgetfulness of self. But in thousands of cases it has been practised for egoistic reasons, being prescribed as

conducive to health. At best, it is a dismal perversion
of aim. Happiness has been taken to mean a prosperous
life on earth, and we have tried to make out that Christ
spoke of prosperity as blessedness. Thus, while recognizing the deadliness of the cult of pleasure, we have
been altruists for ourselves, and hedonists for others:
an absurdity, one would think, which could hardly last.
But it does.

Thus according to Christ's teaching the present distress is due to human life having been ordered on the
wrong lines; man being its centre and not God. It is
an immense encouragement to see that our calamities
are our own fault: for so they are remediable. If they
are not our fault they must be God's fault: and anyone
who seriously believed that would be likely to go
mad.

If then they are remediable, the remedy lies in our
planting in the young generation of to-day a sounder
interpretation of life. All well wishers of mankind are
being brought to see this: though many forget that the
deep and inexhaustible precept uttered by our Lord as
the opening words of His ministry on earth indicate
the fact quite plainly. "Change your minds (about God
and Satan, Heaven and Hell, pleasure and profit, etc.)
for the Kingdom of Heaven is close to you." No wonder
people are saying it is time to try Christianity. Fundamentally, then, the change is for us to regard the glory
of God, that is, the giving of ourselves unstintedly to
Him, to living His Life and to doing His Will, as the
summum bonum; the happiness of man being a corollary,
not an end in itself. But meantime the present distress
is to be our guide. It is not the pain and trouble around
us that are the main stimulus to our compassion; but
the prevailing ignorance of God's nearness: of His

Power, His proffered Love, blended of course with Severity, and His wondrous Patience.

No sooner do we see this truth than our thoughts turn to the children. There lies the hope: for they are still capable of learning: and in this hope the following pages have been written. Our anxieties are not evils to be abolished, but indicators of the true way of serving God: viz. by first learning to know Him through love; then by passing on the knowledge to those whose hearts are still clean: and leaving the results of our efforts whole-heartedly in His hands.

The book is not an attempt to expound even in out-line the Christian Faith: indeed the corporate aspect, the meaning of membership in a Body, is very slightly sketched. The object has been to point out that just when we have learnt the need of unanimity in our educational aims, a deep and unsuspected divergence of principle has been stirring discord and paralyzing our energies. In the recognition of that grave fact there is boundless hope.

LETTERS ON EDUCATION

THE following correspondence is between two men, great friends, though not very closely intimate with each other—James and Henry. Henry, who writes the first letter, is a business man with three children, the eldest being eleven years old, the youngest eight. James is somewhat of a recluse, but a close observer of society and profoundly interested in efforts made for "Reconstruction."

The letters begin towards the end of the Great War.

Letter I

Berkshire,
Aug. 1918.

My dear James,

I daresay you have noticed the curiously sudden increase in educational interest which seems to have spread throughout the country for some little time past. What do you make of it? It has all the appearance of being in some way the outcome of ideas forced upon us by the war, though I own I cannot see any necessary connexion between the two things. Whether we win the war or not, it is perfectly evident that we Britons have borne the brunt of it, and that without it, the cause of Liberty, Justice and Honour would have been lost. But then, if that is a mild way of stating our achievement, look at it in the light of our want of preparation. Why should the public, just as we are showing what we can do, wake up to a new belief in education? Have we not for years, nay always, been a people whose education has been haphazard, ill thought out and wholly unsystematic compared to that of our Continental neighbours? And did not our unprepared condition in 1914 show that we had no genuine belief in study, or in training or scientific thought, applied to the mighty problem of Imperial Defence? Yet we may say now that we have succeeded *à merveille* in spite of our ramshackle ways and mental indolence. How do you explain this ebullition of a faith in education just when the country has given proof on a vast scale that we can accomplish really great things in spite of being a singularly uneducated people? I should have thought that our success would have had just the contrary effect. Do let me know what you think about this. To tell the truth, I am writing in a self-interested fashion, not only as an enquirer into my countrymen's psychology. My little family is presenting me with problems as to their education, which threaten to become uncommonly perplexing in the near future. Jack, the eldest boy, is just going to school, and the H.M. tells me that the curriculum of subjects is determined, not by what he believes to be suitable to little boys, but by what the public schools prescribe in their entrance examinations; and on what principles those examinations are arranged, he has no notion whatever! Indeed, he implied that nobody else had either. Now this is a curious state of things to exist along with an increased faith in education! Are we to believe that our "upper class" boys are trained in a chaotic fashion, at random? If so, where is one to look for any clear guidance?

I hope you won't think these questions a bore. If you are good enough to shed a little light on them, I daresay you won't mind my writing further, on training generally, because not only school education seems to me difficult to understand, but home training is strangely indefinite and amorphous in all classes of society, and I own I am seriously perplexed.

Yours ever,

HENRY.

Letter II

Huntingdonshire,
Aug. 1918.

My dear Henry,

Very glad to hear from you again; nor do I regret in the least that you are perplexed about the training of your children and aghast at the nebulous condition of the country's mind about education and all that hangs upon it. Unless some of us were perplexed, where would be the hope of a remedy? I give you my word, there is scarcely a man worth attending to in this land, who would claim that he knows what education means. The people who profess to know are in deeper darkness than any.

You may have heard that I have been trying to clear some notions on matters of social service by correspondence in the local newspaper. Publicity has compassed me about with a motley group of applicants for advice on matters connected with the training of the young for citizenship. For instance, a peasant woman in these parts wants to know how to bring up twelve children on £2. 10*s*. weekly; the difficulty being that she is at work all day, knows very little, and cannot give ten minutes daily to any kind of teaching or even control. The husband cannot read. Conceive the problem! Yet the parson tells me the children are decidedly easier to manage at school than most of the others, and he puts it down to the mother being obliged in self-defence to insist on obedience, as she has no time to "argufy" and recalcitrance would make life a blank impossibility! When you come to see us, I must show you her two letters. They are truly racy, graphic and sincere, though the vocabulary is small.

Along with this, comes a grave enquiry from a firm of engineers in the Midlands. They are establishing some kind of technical school for youngsters, but are brought up short against a prevailing dislike of steady work. The lads have good brains, as they are carefully picked from secondary schools, but they are indolent mentally, shrinking from anything like concentration as soon as the gritty parts of the subject are reached. The bigwigs suddenly find themselves turned into schoolmasters, and are bewildered no less than other members of that profession. Having learnt to contemplate the Universe as a machine, the ill-starred heads of the firm, the "successful men," have to make provision for young human minds of both sexes; the only thing clear being that all the minds differ from each other; and that the surest sign of a teacher being hopelessly astray is when he is convinced he has hit upon some true method.

Along with these questions comes a letter from Lady Middleditch—such the signature seems to be: but you know what the signatures of busy women are!—a strenuous social worker, whose son is now twenty years old, a very satisfactory specimen in most people's opinion, yet decidedly more interested in himself than in other folk; is likely to make a "good thing" out of his work as a chartered accountant in Leeds, but distresses his altruistic parent by the languor of his interest in her Welfare Committee work and by a growing sense of the importance of £ s. d. At his public school he was much less self-absorbed, being a prefect and a prominent athlete, and keen on running his house well. But now the *ego* is assuming prominence in his cosmos; though the Lady M. words the matter differently. What am I to say to these enquirers?

Do you mind expatiating a little further on your own puzzles?

My hope is to find some principle which will apply to all the problems presented. It is no easy job, but after all that is no reason why it should not be attempted! So in your next, go ahead and spare not; dot *i*'s and cross *t*'s without stint. No matter how murky the landscape is, you have to find a way, and may not stand still. Young people have a way of growing, and however we elders may prate about heredity, their growth is often made or marred by their training. *Vale.*

Yours ever,

JAMES.

Letter III

My dear James,

It is indeed good of you to give so much attention to my perplexities; and I am emboldened thereby to explain them more intimately than I have yet ventured to do to anyone, even to myself. For in truth the flux of opinion among schoolmasters troubles me little in comparison with my own uncertainty what to be at with my own offspring; and as to see a little way into that darkness is my object I will set out plainly where my hopes as a father are befogged in bewilderment.

I want my two boys, and the girl no less, to become good citizens. They will of course have to make their living and I am trying to impress on them the need of hard work and obedience. The elder boy is a good ordinary specimen and will never, I fancy, give any trouble. He shows a practical turn of mind but is quick at book-learning, healthy and well-disposed. The girl, who comes next, is a dear little soul, quite happy in fagging for her brothers. The youngest is an oddity: seems to dislike all practical matters, even machinery, which most boys, I find, passionately love, and is dreamy and imaginative: rhymes a bit, and likes to spin strange yarns out of his head to his sister.

But looking ahead, I see the need of something more definite in the way of character-training. Since the war began we have, many of us, come to see that if this world is to be made a better place there must be a more vigorous and widespread spirit of service; less selfishness; more efficiency. Boys must be made to work and girls must be handy and practical: and for a dreamy sort like Colin there is little or no demand. Thank God, no one of them is likely to be vicious or eccentric, unless it be Colin, who may develop into the latter.

What they all lack is interest in other boys and girls, and in anything to do with history, except of course a few of the old stories. This troubles me, for I believe that without some knowledge of the history not only of England but of other countries as well no young fellow will be a really useful man. It was all very well for you and me to scorn foreigners as we often did forty years ago: but the need of co-operation with foreigners is becoming every year more urgent, and I am not disposed personally to laugh at the yellow peril; nor indeed at American competition. There is a certain amateurishness about our English work which is very likely to be our undoing before many decades have run. We don't believe in thorough training, and it is a perpetual wonder to me that we have got on as well as we have.

In short, I desiderate in my children, a spirit ready to co-operate with foreigners along with a ready response to the spur

of competition. Civilization to-day demands of us both qualities.
But how to induce them I know not: but I do know that if you
cannot advise me no one can.

Ever yours,

HENRY.

Letter IV

My dear Henry,

I think I said something in my last about perplexities
being beneficial. Without perplexities we cannot progress. If we
progress with them, it is because we understand them. They
need to be interpreted; and as they are interpreted they have a
way of vanishing, only to re-appear with a different formula.
They are like the Hebrew occupants of the Roman Ghetto: who
are said to offer you an article at the top of some *calle*, and if the
bargain fails, they re-appear half way down with a more moderate offer, hoping you will not recognize them. All right dealing
with such gentlemen depends on understanding them. So perplexities are to be welcomed because they are to be resolved.

Now you won't mind my putting to you a question or two
to clear the air?

You speak of training the youngsters to aim at co-operation
with foreigners, and to respond to the spur of competition. Are
you sure that the two things are compatible with each other?

Yours ever,

JAMES.

Letter V

My dear James,

To plunge into *medias res*: unless co-operation can be
combined with the keenness stirred by competition, then all I
can say is, this world is played out as a scene for man's habitation.
Rapidity of communication is binding all nations together, and
however difficult it proves to be to establish a League of Nations
it will be done, you will see, not because we are more brotherly
than our fathers, but because there is no alternative that is not
simply hell. But along with this co-operation there must be

stimulus: mankind being so lazy by nature that they will not work except in presence of the abyss of famine. Then, too, you may have heard that the experts calculate on the world becoming congested—that is, giving no room for expansion—in little over 200 years. Though you and I will have moved on, we must make ready for this formidable *dénouement*; and clearly there must be a more vigorous spirit of industry. That, I hold, can only be kept going—anyhow for Englishmen—by the prod of competition.

Isn't this so?

Yours ever,
HENRY.

Letter VI

My dear Henry,

I am very glad to note that your desire is to train your boys to the sense of citizenship; and further that you recognize the spirit of co-operation as essential; and that by co-operation you mean the real thing: partnership or association with *aliens* (as they are now held to be) for the common welfare. Perhaps you hardly perceive what a formidable task you are taking in hand. You are hoping that the lads will forego the belief—universally cherished hitherto in this land—that patriotism for an Englishman means a conviction of our superiority to every foreign nation, and that any scepticism as to that conviction is a disloyalty to our oldest and most sacred traditions. Is it not obvious that this is the very quintessence of arrogance? and that of all national qualities it is the one which most effectually forbids co-operation? Consider, I beg you: what sort of partnership could we ourselves establish with any foreign nation in whom we discerned the same assumption? As a matter of fact there is no European people which has exhibited—I don't say nourished —this arrogance towards Gt Britain so plainly as we have told all of them that we are better than they. Or if you would answer that the Germans were guilty of this very offence in a peculiarly heinous fashion before the war, recollect what we thought of them for doing so. Of course they made their arrogance hideous beyond belief by their barbarities. But that is because the Prussians are a barbarous people: a unique blend of four races:

and I am not explaining our detestation of their un-English temperament, but reminding you that our temperament cannot fail to be unpleasing to them because it is un-German: that is, it exhibits, very plainly, the most offensive quality that we see now has been a Prussian quality for 500 years: namely, an assumption of superiority. Supposing their manifestation of this arrogance had been like our own: gentlemanly, humorous, ironical, and occasionally considerate: well, I suppose we never should have noted it at all. How astonishingly clear to us now is the German national conceit! For centuries how blatant it has been! Their attempts at veiling it, how clumsy and how rare! Why then was it that we failed to mark what these enemies of civilization were doing? Scores of wrong answers have been given to that question. There is only one right one: it is that our conviction of our own superiority was so unassailable, so traditional, so plainly righteous and true, a very token of the favour of Providence and a law of the Universe of things, that we long ago gave up the attempt to imagine how any other people whatsoever could claim a like superiority for themselves. The thing was unbelievable; and even now suppose someone anonymously were to publish his belief that the Americans, for instance, are going to "down us" all by their industry and vast resources, he would be put down as a fool or a foreigner, unless he chose his words with uncommon care. But it is idle to ask what would happen if an Englishman were to say openly that the American or any other nation was finer, better, more admirable than the British; for I gravely doubt if any one of us could put the thought into words: and certainly if he could he wouldn't.

Don't suppose, my good friend, that I am railing against a flaw in other people's temperament from which I conceive my-self to be free. Not for a moment! I freely confess I can't shake off the idea that our assumption of superiority is well-grounded: and that is not because my reason tells me so, but my love does. I see that our love for our country has overset our judgment not so much in giving us the wrong opinion, as in preventing us from being humble. We have a singular gift of veiling from foreign eyes many—perhaps all—of our good characteristics: but our national pride is known to all men. It is so deep and so congenial to us that even if we wished to pose as modest we couldn't keep it up. To do so would require a sustained energy and a histrionic gift which we know Nature has withheld. So we let the matter slide.

All this may be very lovable and very natural and even excusable: but I must point out that it is a fashion which immensely aggravates the task now set to the League of Nations: and also the difficulty of planting the true spirit of co-operation in a young boy.

But forgive me I beg: I have been prosing.

Yours ever,

JAMES.

Letter VII

My dear James,

It is very good of you to take so much trouble and you have deepened my conviction, I will not deny it, of the difficulty of my parental programme; and also of the task before Great Britain, on whose shoulders mainly the League of Nations is likely to rest. We agree in thinking that if civilization is to be saved the League must be a going concern and in short a world-Parliament powerful enough to keep alive and strengthen what we call the spirit of co-operation in place of the spirit of strife. Your point is that to bring up boys to the right spirit means a victory over a deeply-rooted national tradition of something which you call arrogance. Well, I agree: and I think I know how it can be done. Briefly, it must be by training them to be modest boys and free from personal conceit: and there I set great store by our public schools, which, though they are marred by serious defects, are conspicuously successful in teaching a youngster to know his own place. My hope is, then, that my lads will not be of the sort who feed our national arrogance: especially as I think it probable that they will choose careers at home and not be brought much into contact with foreigners.

Then as to your question about reconciling this aim with the exposing of the boys to the stimulus of competition, I am not sure that I see any insuperable difficulty. When you come to think of it, you and I have had plenty of this stimulus, and we have learnt from it the invaluable lesson that to make a success of this world a man must take pains, and more important still must not give way to self-indulgence. I am sure there is a great deal too much relaxation of the old-fashioned discipline in many homes: and I am determined that the boys shall clearly understand that they cannot be the sort of men that I want them to be if they are disobedient to authority, or soft, or sensual, or in the broadest sense of the word, dishonest.

You see, if I can get these ideas into their heads, they will be fortified against the temptations of young manhood, and I should feel pretty confident that they would do good work, if they went into business for instance or took up cattle-ranching. Of course in such a place as the West of Canada one of them might easily be removed far from religious influences. But I should hope that the moral training he is going to receive would pull him through. Some time perhaps you would tell me how far you would rely on religious teaching for the sort of guidance boys like mine will require when they leave home. I ask this on the warrant of the interest you always show in my concerns.

Yours sincerely,

HENRY.

Letter VIII

Dear Henry,

In your letter there is of course much with which I cordially agree. The state of the world urgently calls for characters marked by high aims and practical sagacity. We have to enquire whether your programme gives good hope of success in this great endeavour.

Let us leave the sagacity for the nonce, and ponder on what we mean by high aims.

The human child is always born with over-mastering desires to satisfy his inclinations. In all cases, those inclinations begin by being physical: in short, those of bodily appetite. In many cases the physical desires remain for years the most dominant: and growth in virtue means subjugation of those desires. That is a truism.

But now tell me, before we come to my next proposition. Do we hope for our children that the subjugation shall be complete? Or that it should only proceed as far as it does in the case of the average Englishman?

Then, another question. The above description does not apply to a majority of our children. A very large number will have their tussle in life not with appetite so much as with what we call worldliness: a low, earthly, ideal. They have before them the peril of the slightly swelled head; of craving for comfort; of refined slothfulness; of self-absorption; more subtle foes than the craving for drink; not because they are less objectionable but because they are far more easily concealed: and if concealed as they often are by tact and decorum the world is content to leave well alone. Or, to put it more accurately, these children have to grow to something higher than self-regard. Again, then I ask, do we wish this victory to be complete, or that it should proceed only so far as it does in the case of the average Englishman? For if it is complete it must begin very early. If not, there is no hurry.

Yours in all sincerity,

JAMES.

Letter IX

My dear James,

Some days have gone by since you wrote, and the fact is I have had to scratch my head more than once before being ready with an answer. However, I have it now, and can give it quite shortly: to your first question anyhow. Decidedly, I should wish my boys' victory over sensual desires of all kinds to be complete: short, that is, of anything like crazy asceticism; such as indeed we may read of, but not, in England at least, find in practice.

The second is not so simple. Your batch of bad qualities may be labelled obnoxious kinds of selfishness. Pride and the like, as I have said, the public school will stamp out. But there is a sort of honourable ambition in which I should be sorry to see my boys lacking. I may be wrong, but there seems to me to be less of that kind of keenness than there was—leaving the war out of account as being wholly exceptional.

Is this fairly clear?

Yours ever,

HENRY.

Letter X

My dear Henry,

Clear? Yes. But your letter prompts another question which is nearer still to the centre of the subject. Only I must embark on an explanation first.

We are up against an ambiguity in this matter of completeness of self-conquest. Some principle must be discovered on which you draw a distinction between sensuality and pride. Supposing a young man finds he can't bridle the flesh without asceticism, is he to be condemned for practising it? It is conceivable that his desires may be unusually strong. Is he wrong, then, in giving up wine or even meat, so as to be quit of an impediment to his movements in the combat with his enemy? It will save trouble if I give you my notion and you can tell me how far you agree.

Asceticism or self-discipline may be healthy or unhealthy in the same way and for the same reason as ambition may be a good or a very poisonous quality. In both cases it depends on whether the aim is self-regarding or is directed to something ideal, that is higher than the self. Thus a middle-aged man may recognize that he has been largely a failure owing to his subjection to appetite: and he thereupon makes a lot of rules about abstinence and bores his friends to tears and worries his hostesses because no one knows what he is going to eat or drink next: and what is far worse he descants to all and sundry on the benefits he derives from a fad. Notice then that it is the old enemy self-improvement which spoils everything, and self-complacency which makes the idiotic assumption that improvement has been achieved. So with ambition. We admire the strenuousness of our mutual friend Hambledown, but it is all tarred with the brush of self-love: he cannot conceal his desire for applause, and the poor fellow struts and strains his best, failing in gaining approval because he seeks it: like a painstaking but self-conscious actor.

Thus whether men's infirmities be of sensuality or pride all efforts at amendment are nothing worth in so far as self-regard is the motive power. If you agree with me, you will correct a fallacy in your distinction between the two classes of infirmity: viz. that the one should be treated by extirpation, the other by emollients, dressings and the like, so that they be mitigated to the degree allowed by public opinion.

Yours ever, JAMES.

Letter XI

Dear J.,

On the whole, though not without some hesitation, I concede your point. That is to say, there is an honourable ambition which no young man should be without; but if it is to be worthy of honour there must be nothing—or as little as possible—of self in it. Further, there might be a good deal of self in it without the silly world detecting it: so that in so far as that goes, public opinion is a bad test. Yes: I would agree there.

But as a practical man I demur somewhat. Are we parents and all schoolmasters on the wrong tack in appealing to a boy's natural desire to develop his own powers; to assert his own individuality and, in short, to make the best of himself? Cast an eye on our schoolboys—and schoolgirls too for that matter—and are you going to rely on an appeal to what you call "something ideal"? My notion is, this lofty kind of appeal would be something premature when made far and wide among our young folk. Nor do I suppose for a moment that if there had been nothing of ordinary ambition in men like Drake, Chatham, Warren Hastings, Nelson, etc., our Empire would ever have been built up. What am I to make of this?

Ever yours,
H.

Letter XII

Dear H.,

I thought you would launch this bolt upon me. It certainly is not unexpected and it will be my fault if it finds a chink in my cuirass.

There appears to be a clash of interests where yet our moral consciousness tells us that both are right. Thus (1) wherever self is visibly the motive of action, the action loses its virtue. Yet the reward of right action is the development, the expansion, of the self. How then can you avoid appealing to the natural self-love, if you wish your youngster to develop his powers? (2) Is there anything so very wrong in a reasonable self-culture?

(1) This is simple. Suppose a family of nine brothers growing

up: all extremely self-centred except one who is remarkably unselfish or self-forgetful: always helping the others and never insisting on his own rights. Certainly for him the personality will develop while for others it will pine. This rudimentary but profound truth of psychology is the answer to "patriotic" objections to the League of Nations. If Great Britain learns to help other nations she will become greater. The longer we remain narrow in our interests the less we grow.

(2) The poison of self-culture—no matter how reasonable, how enlightened, how successful—is beyond all words deadly. I can't tell you why! it lies too deep and works for a long time unseen, but generally stimulates a hunger in the soul, and if it does not, but leaves the soul contented, there is no death so complete. The commonest symptom of the hunger is the desire for excitement, which allows us to forget ourselves for a time. Vice, too, is a perverted form of escaping from the self: drunkenness, for example, obviously so: lust less obviously; gambling a most hideous attempt to flee from self while all the time pampering it most subtly. This is the only vice which destroys the natural affections completely. But I suppose there is no sort of active viciousness which is not more hopeful than the contentment of stagnation. Desire, however perverted, is after all a sign of life and in a sense objective. But introspection bred of indifference to our fellow men and to Nature, art, etc., is worse, and induces insanity. In its early stages the desire to escape from self shows itself in mild ways thought to be not only innocent but beneficial, such as perpetually reading light stuff, or adding the excitement of competition to bodily exercise; matches to games, etc. And so on.

Sincerely yours,
J.

Letter XIII

My good friend: you are beginning to face me with posers. Hence again a delay of a few days before my answering. Undoubtedly this question of self-forgetfulness is vital to our enquiry, and must be faced in the way Talleyrand said Wellington talked French: "avec beaucoup de courage." It may be that further reflection on it will lead to new and interesting issues in the theory of training the young.

Your explanation illuminates the matter, but still, if I may say so, it strikes me as rather too abstract, and we must be very careful to view hard facts as hard facts and not as arguments for a thesis. But I am a child in these matters. Could they not have taught us a little philosophy at Cambridge?

You see: here the shoe pinches. Every schoolmaster tells me the same thing—that, whatever be the reason, the large majority of our boys and a great many even of our girls are intellectually inert; they come to school fairly on the *qui vive*, being still children, but something at fourteen or fifteen years of age arrests their desire to learn, and upon some 75 per cent. steals the stolidity of our race. Now I must save my boys from this if possible. The question then is, are the dangers to character which you say belong to the appeal to young ambitions so certain as to warrant us in foregoing the stimulus which that appeal can alone supply? If at fifteen they lose all wish to learn, why, bless me! they will miss nearly all the equipment for life which education is meant to give, and moreover will be dull companions for us elders in our time of decline. Their loss will mean loss for others. Are we justified in running any such risk?

Ever yours,
H.

Letter XIV

H., my incautious friend, you are opening the gates of a sluice, and a tidy volume of pent-up waters is on the move.

Can we agree on this question? Granting, as I understand you do, that self-forgetfulness in presence of an ideal is the true principle of life for man to live on, but hesitating about all of its applications in the face of practical demands: which are we to say? (*a*) That the principle is to be acted on for its own sake, that is, because in itself it is right and good, or (*b*) because it is expedient; that is, makes life happier? You will observe that you doubt both. I mean that you would shrink from pinning your faith out and out to either. (*a*) you would uphold as a desirable practice unless it conflicts, as it would seem to, with (*b*) expediency. Now the difficulty of education is that in early years the divergence between these two is far from manifest, and most of us have been brought up on a kind of Mazawattee blend dating from thirty (or more) years ago. The only way to grip the truth is to note how the two programmes work out: remembering all along that whichever is right, there is no sort of doubt which of the two is the more painful, and which therefore in the comparison starts heavily handicapped.

Selfishness, or ego-centricity we all know to be deadly in an individual. But so it is in a family. You know how some families achieve a fine standard of unity among their own members but contrive to fancy themselves as better than other families, and *pro tanto* all is spoilt. Look at it next among nations. It is a truism that patriotism has been lauded and preached and taught to children as a prime virtue: and that it means the desire for the welfare of our own nation; far stronger than the desire for the welfare of other nations, indeed excluding the latter completely. How has it worked? Devilishly—there is no other word for it. The nations, as civilization spread, became more and more united externally by commerce, that is by growing identity of interests, but along with that and spurred by it they have been infected with the ego-centric spirit of competition, and the result is Pandemonium, or the rendering the whole of this interesting little planet of ours uninhabitable. Of course our way of pursuing self-interest, being British, seemed in our eyes to be on a higher plane than the German way, and doubtless it was more humane, but it was just as self-centred.

Tell me then if you assent to these bald propositions so far.

Yours ever,

J.

Letter XV

Dear James,

I am in a quandary, so much I freely admit; out of my depth, in short, but perhaps if I give good heed to what you write I may get back to *terra firma* without much floundering.

The connexion between your letter and the training of my lads is not at once apparent, but I suppose lies herein: that if self-forgetfulness or self-sacrifice is a law of individual conduct, children must be so trained as to recognize it, welcome it, and practise it. Further that if the law holds good for the individual, it must ultimately be binding on nations, so that the great principle meets us again and again whether the child is being reared for a quiet "private" life or for the turmoil of international politics.

So far, so good. But the *tenebrae* descend again when I think of the limits of the self-sacrifice to which we are bidden. It is clear there must be limits. The boys are not going to walk about in rags and live on a dry crust, any more than this Empire is going to give up valuable pieces of territory or coaling stations merely out of brotherhood. But for the life of me I cannot see how the line is to be drawn. It is one more instance of the difficulty of applying the principle we hear on Sundays to the daily work of the week; of bringing the Sermon on the Mount down into the bowels of Cheapside; which so far are not exactly bowels of compassion only. Unless you can show me this I fear we are no "forrarder."

Ever yours,
H.

Letter XVI

My dear H.,

It is not easy to concentrate attention upon ethical problems when Europe is seething in the cauldron, but you set me a good example, so I will stick close to your question.

I find it necessary at this point to appeal to the example of Christ. This is not as Christian doctrine or theology—don't be alarmed—but purely as a matter of ethics, I must direct your attention to a most impressive fact. Have you observed of late how the increased communication between distant peoples has revealed the immensity of the gulf that yawns between differently coloured races; a gulf which there seems no prospect of our ever spanning. There seems to be no department of life, no set of principles, no ideas of duty or of righteousness which, as ideas, command assent among most Eastern and Western peoples alike. In fact, is it not the case that there is agreement on one point only: that is, in reverence for the character of Christ? Now let us leave on one side numerous and weighty considerations as to the hope that herein lies for the future unification of mankind; I want to point out that the unanimity of reverence accorded to this character is due to the completeness, the thoroughness, with which Christ ignored and set aside the egocentric principle of living and subordinated it always to a higher law. What that was we will consider later. When I say thoroughness I mean that there is no sign that in thought He never hesitated a moment in pursuing the *Via dolorosa;* just as the enthralling thing in the example of many martyrs is not the pain endured but the buoyancy of spirit or thoughtfulness for others shown in the hour of agony.

Next comes the paradox that in proportion as the self is suppressed the personality gains in power. That is to say that if Christ or Paul or Francis or any other transcendently great character had in any one particular drawn a line and refused to let the self-abnegation go further, all would have been lost—the careers would have become mere records of men differing from scores of others only in degree, whereas now we have the entire principle on which the most dazzling counterfeit of the Christian life is based, wholly set aside; and therein lies the spell of the character, the power of the personality.

Lastly, another paradox; that though mankind acknowledges the beauty, the power, the divinity of the wholly selfless character, there has been no period in history when the mass of mankind—very nearly all—has not imitated the counterfeit. They have insisted on some self-abnegation; sometimes on a good deal, but whenever it has shown signs of going on to completeness, it has roused opposition, has been thought to be more or less mad, and not till after death has it been recognized as the "real thing."

Do you agree? This is not a mere Biblical matter, but concerns our every day life.

Yours ever,

J.

Letter XVII

Excuse a p.c., as any gentleman in these days must. I cannot make head nor tail of your last unless you give illustrations; and don't forget we are concerned with children.

H.

Letter XVIII

Dear H.,

Your card, though marked by the "soul of wit," gives me just the cue I want. In the following remarks, then, I try to appeal to convictions which you and all sensible folk, *boni homines*, Cicero used to call them, hold in common.

Tom, Dick and Harry and other progenitors of children, are pretty well aware of the fact that each child is an immortal soul born into a world whose laws govern in a wondrous uniformity; yet the child is a new thing, different from all others, incalculable, surpassingly fresh and pleasing; but created for a destiny which no man may picture or describe. All that we know about it is that it depends on a free option which the child cannot avoid making during his life on earth.

Dimly and with fitful insight, the fathers of children and the mothers may be said to know so much. What they do not know, except here and there in dwindling number, is that for each child a drama begins soon after birth fraught with unspeakable issues for bliss or woe. That is to say that the child inherits a nature which appears to be completely under the dominion of many propensities and desires, and all of them can be described as selfish, or directed to the gratification of the self; though some of them are fair and comely, others being ugly and baneful and, as it were, poisonous in their working. The difference, however, between the comely and the ugly desires does not reach below the surface. Both classes are equally selfish, and if so, equally to be curbed and subdued, or else they will drag the soul downwards into ruin. Thus the peril of the position is that whereas all the selfish desires are poisonous because they are selfish, some of them seem to be sound and smack of the radiant healthiness of childhood, yet these require in reality quite as stern a treatment as the others.

But what am I doing? Your pithy post-card called for illustrations, and I am only piling on you fresh disquisitions. Listen then to an instructive story.

Years ago, singular fact!—I was a boy at school. Adolescent not yet adult, I made a friend of a contemporary also eighteen years of age, who in modern parlance would be described as a "good sort." He was genial and lenient towards others' peculiarities; the secret of which tolerance was discovered by a remark he made to me—who would think it?—just forty-nine years ago. "Look here," said he, "do you notice that though some people are called good and some bad they are all alike in one respect, viz. they all pursue pleasure; that which pleases them. You happen to like strenuous games and books, others foreign travel, or work among the poor, and so on. Others for the same reason take to drink or roystering or combat, that is to say, they have a fancy for these pastimes. Now my fancy is for 'slacking'; I can't see the fun of all this effort, so I mean to take life uncommonly easy and I am bothered if I shall mind who blames me—for undoubtedly they will be pleasing themselves, and you may be sure I shan't blame them." Poor fellow! he did not make much of a success of this life, and some years ago passed beyond the Veil. I learned at the time "his great language and caught his clear accents": these I have imperfectly reproduced, but the sentiment was exactly as I have given it.

To what does this record point? No careful parent would be quite comfortable if he overheard his son diagnosing humanity as X did in 1872. But the question is whether parents do not so present life to their children as to make it all but impossible for them to diagnose it otherwise. What was wrong with X? You would say that he lumped all inclinations into one category; whereas he ought to have known that even sport is better than slacking, politics better than sport (are they?), philanthropic work the best of all. Yes, but you fail to see that the difference which the world recognizes between one line of life and another is a sham difference, being outward only and insignificant as compared with the deeper classification, which is this:

Every year brings to the growing child a multitude of choices which can't be avoided. He makes them according as he has begun to interpret life, either according to his inclinations or from the higher law of duty, or from a mixture of the two. By the last I mean when duty is put before the boy as a desirable thing for the reward it will bring; (his profession, for instance, is recommended to him for what it will bring him in the way of friends or money or power or health or reputation;) studiedly and most effectively as an opportunity for deepening his conviction that life is a stage, an arena, for getting what you want. Or the work of life, the making a livelihood, is talked of as service—often a most questionable view of it—and it is openly assumed that when the office door is closed behind him young Dick Roe may, or indeed ought, to think of nothing but amusement. That is what I mean by the drawing of the line. A certain concession to public opinion which disapproves of slacking, is prudent, and so is sanctioned by an enlightened selfishness. But why is it disapproved of? Because the public are vaguely aware that a slacker is a person who consumes more than his share of the earth's produce which he does nothing to increase. Again, observe, the moral judgment of the world is based on the assumption which dominated political economy at one time, viz. that everybody is out to get all he can out of life. Many parents make no bones about it; they are unabashed in the example they set as they have never been taught any other, and quite solemnly look on any advocate of a higher life as a fool. But our concern is with the large horde of well-intentioned parents who cannot see that, apart from the Gospel precept about God and Mammon, a life started on this sort of principle of first settling the needs of the ego and then thinking about the happiness of others is a life doomed to miserable and deepening gloom. The description of it will not be impugned by anyone who grasps what a glorious thing life might be for all of us, or how palpably evident it is that the outcome of this baneful compromise is lamentation, mourning and woe for the whole world.

Now I must stop. Note the point reached, and see if you agree: that when people say (as thousands have been saying) that for centuries and among all nations Mammon worship has been supreme, they ought to include in their indictment *all bondage to inclination*—(no matter how much it is condoned by the world) —*which is made the ruling motive of living*, and if so they may find themselves in harmony with the teaching of the Gospel, or anyhow on the way to it. Of that more anon.

Yours ever,

J.

Letter XIX

Well, my dear J., you are laying it on thick now, I must say, and very soon I shall have some fine conundrums to launch back. If your last contention is sound it is plain that the education of 98 per cent. of our children will have to be scrapped, and that is a large order.

Yet, in theory again, and provisionally, so to speak, I admit it. Certain forms of conduct are praised by the world, other forms are condemned, yet among those who practise the former there may be many men thoroughly selfish. True, and the corollary is that the opinion of the world is no guide. But the moment I reach that conclusion, I am brought face to face with the bankruptcy of modern ethics. If the universal opinion of society is erroneous, whither is a bewildered father to turn? The Gospel teaching is jejune and obscure, and besides you say yourself it is in harmony with man's deepest instincts. So if your reasoning runs counter to the instincts, it traverses the Gospel as well. What have you to say to that?

Ever yours,

H.

Letter XX

Dear H.,

Your question is thoroughly pertinent, and I was hoping you would put it. If in my last I had said the last word your objection would be fatal. But now look at this. Hitherto we have both implied that because mankind have spent their energies and concentrated their hopes on trying to treat God and self (Mammon) with equal respect, therefore they really believe they are on an equality, and that as regards the opposite principle taught in the Gospel, we have at large and with an irresistible unanimity discarded it as untrue. But this cannot be. How are we to explain that in the midst of our groping along the moral labyrinth, in steadfast pursuit of temporal goods, we never can resist paying unstinted homage to those—if there are any—who act unassumingly and genuinely on the opposite principle—that is, as if those goods were utter trash in comparison with something higher?

For instance, recall to your mind the atmosphere of 1913 and take careful note, not of the amount of vice or the imminence of civil war or the ghastly disparity of material resources in the country—these were but trifles—but of the prevalence and power of the feeling that suffering of all kinds is an intolerable evil; selfish people engaged in eliminating it from their own lives, unselfish people from other people's lives; but all alike agreeing in their view of sacrifice as tantamount to loss and therefore an evil. Well, then, what happened in October, 1914? A million of our young men came forward cheerfully, welcoming the very thing which the mass of the nation was engaged in banishing as far away as possible; and any stranger would surely have expected us to deride these fellows as a swarm of lunatics. Did we? We did not; and if anyone showed the least inclination to disparage their conduct in the slightest degree we loaded him with unmeasured vituperation. Remember, it was not because they defended our homes—though they did—but because they scouted the notion of suffering being a deterrent—because they welcomed it as a joy, because they stamped upon the damnable creed that what a man sacrifices is lost. It is easy to belittle their action by imputing cheap motives or prating about the herd-instinct. The fact remains unassailably true that they manifested a spirit the direct contrary to that to which we were all enslaved—the spirit of giving all, instead of grabbing what they could; for it was not so much that they offered all that life could give, but that they offered it with the zest and boyish gladness of heroes unconscious of their heroism yet set on the road which leads to the true goal of life. But the more we admired them for their spirit the more we condemned ourselves for our own.

So you see, I avoid your dilemma. It looked in 1913 as if man's deepest instincts sanctioned an interpretation of life which is the flat contradiction of the Gospel. I point out that they were not the deepest instincts. Man, in short, wants to do what is right, but he is incurably muddled-headed. He knows quite well the difference between God and Mammon. When he sees the deeds of those who gaily but without "swank" give to the claims of God a clear and decisive primacy, he recognizes in a moment the only true life and cannot withhold his admiration. Yet when the moment is passed he turns again to his sordid quests and discarded vanities, utterly unsuspicious that having been shown

how to live, he is plunging back into his quagmire of mingled
selfishness and sacrifice.

It is not the foundation instincts that are wrong, but the in-
vincible belief of our countrymen that, whereas in matters of
eternal import and unvarying law two and two do really make
four, the prudent man will act as if they frequently made five.

Now the problem before you and others in education is
simply this: how to still the braying of the donkey in man's
breast. This faculty of English people of behaving towards contra-
dictory claims upon his allegiance, as if they were equally true or
equally false—he never knows which—is beyond all words fatal
to all right conduct of life, and it coexists in wondrous wise with
an unshakable conviction that one is paramount over the other.

And then we wonder at foreigners not understanding us!

Forgive prolixity; you see I must be sure as to your hopes for
your children before I get ready my prescription.

Yours sincerely,

JAMES.

Letter XXI

My dear James,

You certainly waxed a little warm in your last and perhaps
strayed a little from the matter in hand. But I admit it is re-
freshing to come across something clear and unqualified in the
way of an opinion, in these days of half-lights and mixed notions
and slushy talk. A good lady once said to me at dinner (before
the war), "I think the Germans are a better nation than the
French—*in a way*." That is all the guidance I can get in
Lombard Street on anything really important. It is always
qualified by "in a way." As Corney Grain used to say when
called on at a country house to express an opinion on one of his
host's horses, being profoundly ignorant of horseflesh: "That's
a good hock—in its way; so that if it should turn out to be a
bad hock, I can explain that it is not in the way I meant." Certainly old C. G. was not of much use as to the training of the
young. Yet I wish the modern pundits were half as amusing.

Now let's focus the question again. You say the only true
method of living is that of unstinted self-giving for an ideal. I
objected that the world has decided otherwise. You reply that

this decision is hollow; society's deepest convictions sanction the stern creed, but society is always excusing itself for flouting its true beliefs and pursuing what it knows to be a lie. I suppose there is no gainsaying this indictment. But I am still inclined to take up the cudgels for what I should reckon as the best and most civilized ideal of the ordinary good citizen; such a life as that of our friend Anthony—which seems to me really desirable and worthy of imitation in times like these, but yet plainly very different from your self-sacrificing life. Let me picture it briefly.

He was born of fairly well-to-do parents but had to make his livelihood. Was sent to a good school and did well, learnt how to work and grew up with some real love of literature and even of art; passed high into the Indian Civil Service and gave the best years of his life to the government and administration of our great Eastern empire. Is pensioned off and comes home not to live as an idle gossip at Cheltenham or Bedford, but settles down as a country gentleman in a modest way, and for twenty years was the most useful man in the neighbourhood; a solid, sagacious citizen with no axe to grind, but never losing his grasp of public affairs. Meantime his home was a home of culture and refinement, and his three boys bid fair to follow in their father's footsteps and develop into that kind of strong, quiet servant of the community whom society delights to honour.

That is the sort of man I want my boy to be. It would not be quite so easy to describe the aim of a girl's training; but let this suffice as a test of your canon of education. The world respects such a character as Anthony. Is the world wrong? Such men have built up and maintained our Empire, and its good work is their work. You will have a job of it if you mean to dissuade the country from putting them on a pedestal and bidding our youngsters copy them. *Your* ideal man is a very different sort of customer; more of the Sermon-on-the-Mount type I freely admit; but isn't it pretty generally agreed nowadays that that type is no longer possible? Modern conditions require something less sublime; something more self-assertive, not so meek nor so undiscriminating in their charity. I agree with someone—a bishop, I fancy—who said that any nation that ordered its life according to the Sermon on the Mount would be ruined straightway. It cannot be right to let your country sink into ruin.

Therefore it seems to me what we want for ordinary life is a kind of teaching less exalted than the Gospel's; on the same line, so to speak, but not going so far. But this is just what you won't have. I greatly look forward to your answer.

Yours sincerely,

H.

Letter XXII

My dear H.,

Dim memories of Plato remind me of old Socrates addressing himself to what you faithfully describe as "a job of it"; for you have made it clear that the best worldly ideal of modern citizenship, though most attractive, is not the Christian ideal, and therefore one or the other must go. Till we settle which, we are no nearer to solving your difficulty.

Before bringing the Gospel into the question we should notice that a formidable indictment lies against the world's programme: viz. that it has been tried for centuries and has failed. Moreover that so far from the Christian ideal being discredited, during the stress of late years, why, it has never been tried; but there has been an unmistakable demand for a "return to Christ"; that is, that thousands of hard-headed men who know and care nothing about the fundamentals of the matter are in theory loyal to Christian ethics, and recognize more clearly than ever before that in that ethics lies the one hope of humanity. Of course there are millions who see nothing of the kind, and history will depend on which point of view prevails.

Now let me venture on your forbearance. Instead of my answering your letter, let me refer you to one or two already sent from this study, for you to think over. You won't mind. I want to cry 'Pax' for a bit.

Yours ever,

J.

Letter XXIII

(After some weeks)

Dear J.,

Most fortunately I have been having a slack time in the City, and have given some hours a day to wrestling with the holiday task you set me. I trust you are the better for a trip in a very charming country, and are fortified for some more of my mystifications.

Till lately I confess I looked vaguely on Christian teaching as confirmatory of the world's general idea of virtue; a busy altruism coupled with a reasonable amount of self-interest, seeing that if all the educated classes adopted such a line of life, probably things would go very much better than they do. But fresh study of the Bible convinces me that there is some deep divergence between this citizenship ideal and that to which Christ called His followers. So much I can see. But I can't pretend to have made out what this Christian life or ideal really is. It is a singular fact that after forty-five years of living as an ordinary sort of professing Christian I should have to confess to so blank an ignorance; for in discerning my own plight I suddenly become aware of the same darkness enveloping thousands of my fellow men. "You English," said a distinguished foreigner, "are sinking under the complexity of your civilization, and the worst of it is that you are losing hold of the fundamentals." Weighty words, James. The only point in them which seems to me disputable is that implied in "losing hold," for I have doubts whether we English ever began to take hold. Certainly *I* never did; and except yourself is there anyone we know who is facing fairly the question: "Why was I brought into the world?"

My good friend—my only stand-by in the shadows and the storm—let me thank you for your readiness to hold out a guiding hand. Life is hard to understand indeed; but it is not so dark as it was, and in my very fact of bewilderment I am beginning to discover the dawn of a new light. I know I can reckon on your help.

Here is the boggle. We have two instincts of moral consciousness within us too powerful to be ignored; the desire for self-improvement and the desire to help others. Every right-minded man, surely, is bound to act upon both, seeing that for him neither can be withstood. Why, then, is it so fatal (according to your reading of the Gospel) if we put the things essential to self-improvement as the first objects of our endeavours; a good home to live in; sufficient food and clothing; a circle of friends; a fair education and some intellectual tastes? It is true no doubt that we are tempted to give an excessive attention to such things, and a vast number of us succumb; failing to learn the truth even from the miseries of the war. But somehow the N.T. keeps on talking as if it were not a question of degree only, but a total reversal, denial and extirpation of all that the mass of people set before themselves as desirable—wealth, friends, home comforts, children and the like—even fame as a reward for a devoted life.

Again: starting from the two instincts mentioned above, what am I to think of the enormous disproportion of failure compared with success in social efforts? Can anything be more bewildering than a study of social progress now or at any time in the past? Some years ago there was a leader in *The Times* quietly facing the possibility that all our schemes for social betterment have failed, are failing, and are destined to fail again.

There's a cheerful look out! Now I remember the same journal remarking about Lord Shaftesbury that he was perhaps the only man of the century of whom you could undoubtedly say that his work in life had made man happier. What a grim verdict! Think of all the effort! Contrast the strenuousness of our social activities to-day with the callous acquiescence of 100 years ago, and then tot up the gains; and you cannot say for certain that there are any at all. If I turn to self-improvement it is even worse; the more attention I give to my character-training the less able I am to do or to be what I want. And everybody else is in much the same hole, most of them anxious to do what is right, but in a regular muddle of thought, groping blindly, jostling painfully, stumbling piteously along a road which is neither broad nor easy, and yet has all the air of leading to destruction.

We have in short tried for centuries the method of acquiescence, of shrugging the shoulders (the one expressive gesticulation we retain), of casualness and "waiting till the clouds roll by," and so forth; and now that we try the only alternative our failure is more dismal and more patent than ever, simply because it dogs *all* our steps and compasses us whether we move or whether we stand still, or sit and twist our thumbs or lie down and woo slumber. If now and again and here or there some improvement may be descried it never can be traced to human foresight and agency with any reassuring certainty, nor does it tell us how to

face the future of which we know nothing except that it will
be unlike the past.

What a muddle it all is! Yet people bid us hope! even the
Dean of St Paul's says it is a duty for Christians; but neither he
nor anyone that I can hear of gives any hint *what* we are to
hope for, or from what quarter we are to look for a cure for all
this conglomeration of ills.

I hope I have explained the symptoms of the modern epidemic
fairly clearly. I can well understand that in your, so to speak,
Euganean Hills the fever of modern unrest is less oppressive.
By the way W. S. calls it "life's *fitful* fever"; but if fitful means
sporadic or intermittent it won't do as an epithet for to-day. Our
fever is not sporadic, it is everywhere; nor intermittent, for it
never stops.

Yours with much gratitude,
HENRY.

Letter XXIV

My dear Henry,

Let me say at once that your words hint at the deepest
darkness being, as it often has been, the herald of the day. If
you were not in perplexity you would indeed be without hope.
Things being what they are, *humanum est errare*. As soon as we
are born we "go astray and speak lies"; but salvation begins
directly we know that we are on the wrong road, and thank
goodness! so far you have certainly got. Heaven begins for us
with a change of thought.

For instance, take the failure of a huge percentage of practical effort, to which you have so feelingly alluded. Notice how
we refuse to learn from Christ's story that visible, temporal,
worldly, success is no test whatever of the truth of our aim. We
habitually make it the one test, and then, of course, are at the
mercy of circumstances, results, changes and chances, untraceable causes, the infirmities of others. But why not learn from
all whose wills have been brought into subjection to God's will
that a duty once discerned is a signal from Heaven for thanks-
giving, and especially is this the case when it is seen to involve
suffering, self-mortification or what we call failure? How striking

is the combination of joyous confidence in the perception of the divine guidance, and the anticipation of terrible obstacles in St Paul's words: "For a great door and an effectual is opened unto me, and there are many adversaries." "Adversaries" in those days was a synonym for failure plus persecution; the being silenced by being torn in pieces or stoned, or clapped into prison for two years and chained perhaps to a sulky and barbarous Syrian. Paul treats the failure as a sign of his having co-operated with God, not as a failure in our sense at all; and the sufferings likewise; they are symptoms of the Narrow Way and that is the only important fact about them. To mention their painfulness would have been impossible to that glorious soldier of Christ. The only injunction he gives about hardships is "Endure them."

I daresay my long letter was discursive. Forgive. Instead then of summarizing what I have written let us concentrate on this last point. The want of visible success in social work ought not to be a depressing fact at all. I think you will agree that the Bible teaches this; but I suspect you will say that in that case the Bible is no use for the twentieth century, and moreover that what people say about the Will of God being sufficient for us is far from convincing. You will see that if we can agree about this we shall be a good step nearer to agreement as to our training of boys and girls, or rather children, for it concerns them first and foremost.

Ever yours sincerely,

J.

Letter XXV

James, my good friend. I am glad your anticipation was what it was, as it gives me some confidence that I shall not be writing undiluted rubbish to-day. Latterly, in handling these deep matters I have been afraid you must at times have been reminded of that racy verse in Ecclus. (ch. xxii): "He that telleth a tale to a fool speaketh to one in a slumber; when he hath told his tale he will say 'What is the matter?'" But I recognize and greatly appreciate your patience.

Yes, on the whole, I should make the objection you mention. That is to say, if the Bible teaches something contrary to general moral experiences I should say so much the worse for the Bible; we don't any longer think it is all equally inspired, and any teaching which straightly contradicts experience will be rightly discarded.

But wait a moment. We are thinking over the lack of visible success in social service, Church work and the like. Now I am trying to give full weight to the central principle of self-forget-fulness and in so doing I notice that a great deal of so-called social service deserves to fail because it is shoddy from the outset. Years ago many smart people took up social work among the poor, either as a fashionable craze, or as a sort of self-defence against a danger, or as a means of display; and even if their motive was benevolent their tone smacked just enough of con-descension to make failure certain. And they deserved to fail. Clearly, if it is to succeed, there must be no selfish aim.

But supposing there is not, I can't away with your very de-pressing theory that failure is to be none the less expected, and if it comes is to be rejoiced over. That, I hold, is, as the American said, piling it up a bit too mountainous. For instance: What can be so infernal as our failure to solve the Housing Problem? Any fool can see that it is at the bottom of our social disorder because it makes decent home life impossible; and any decay of our home life cuts at the very vitals of the nation's well-being. Other failures could be mentioned equally distressing. Do you really mean to say we can stomach this kind of thing without minding? If so, how are you going to get people to make any effort to remedy the evil? I can't acquiesce in any theory which will perpetuate disease corroding the inner life of old England.

Yours ever,
H.

Letter XXVI

My dear H.,

You have come to an objection to my optimistic creed which is tantamount to the problem of evil. Why should man be confronted with failure in his *good* endeavours? We can stomach the abortiveness of effort which is half-hearted and insincere. But when, after a good deal of stripping off of bandages from the mind's eye, and painful probing, we clearly see the centre of our

disorders to be in the home, has not man a right to expect some
undeniable benefit from the efforts and self-sacrifice, committees, swollen rates, overworked Parliament, toil, voluntary and
compulsory, into which we have plunged for the last fifty years?

Well, note that if he has this right, it carries with it the right
to say and believe that in the case of our generation at least
Creation has been a failure. This is a strong statement. Meantime a jotting or two.

If human life is meant to be simply a striving after a good time
which never comes, I throw up the sponge. The God who so
ordered things has made a mess of this world. Just as we think
we have a solution of our troubles it crumbles away. Thus we
learnt that war is the ordered and inevitable sequel of sin, and
therefore must be the purging away of sin. But it is just not that.
Society is as self-seeking as if the retreat from Mons had never
been. So much just to show that I am not shirking your difficulty,
but emphasizing it.

Suppose, however, that the purpose of our present life is not
happiness but character, and that the more unintelligible our
failures and distresses are, the better we are strengthened "in
the inner man"; what then?

That would involve the admission that life would be too
simple and our discipline too watery if every calamity brought
a visible gain. We should be relying on "a sign." Suppose then
that *the failure of calamity to work a cure* be an evidence not of
the failure of law, but of the malignity of sin which causes
calamity: what then?

Yours,
J.

Letter XXVII

My dear James,

I gather from your last that you are going to deal with two
puzzles later. Be sure and tackle them in your best manner. They
are, in brief, these: How are we to face recurrent failure in such
undertakings as the Housing, where failure means moral
deterioration among innocent people? The second I have not
yet put, but sooner or later it must be faced.

I note from your "jottings" that you will draw your answer
from religion. Now keeping in mind our children and their re-

quirements I find myself faced with an alternative: to use every endeavour either to train them to the religious type, or to the best lay type, there being a marked difference between the two. I am ready to admit that the high ethical standard which you forcibly advocate postulates a religious background, so it is in no hostile spirit that I must point out how superior to your ordinary religious men many of our best laymen are.

These are the heroes of action, the men who approach the ideal of western Europe, characters who take us by storm, being lovers of goodness and—so at least I say—more delightful, suasive, potent for good in that they are intelligible to us all. I mean the great soldier type—simple hearted and wondrously strong, set on duty and in very truth more oblivious of self than your religious man, because his lacking the peculiar mysterious thing you speak of saves him from self consciousness and from that kind of introspective shyness which rightly alienates the mystic minded men from the "ordinary" run of sterling sturdy citizens.

It is here that what people call the lay mind is at issue with the parson's. Among a deal of drivel talked on this subject I welcome a fragment of truth. Nothing will persuade me that these noble fellows who yet have never gained a strong personal hold on religion, are far from the Kingdom of Heaven.

Yours ever,

HENRY.

Letter XXVIII

Dear Henry,

Your first question is postponed. As for your non-religious hero, I hold that the conquest of self is such a marvellous triumph and the effect on character so sublime that in reality the line ought to be drawn—not between believers and unbelievers, in the usual sense, but—between the selfish and unselfish; even though some of the former be Communicants and some of the latter professing Atheists. The question for each and all is how steadfastly we have followed the best light that has been given. Doubtless the lamps are not alike, and some boys are apparently destitute of the ear for God as others are for music. But in all these matters the sense is latent, but it is there.

I must again postpone my answer.

But you are right in saying I am coming to Religion in time. Many will take this to mean only the teaching of Christ, and, as to that, hear my little parable.

Once there was a man standing by a roadside, intent on raising a huge stone that lay before him. Never mind why he was keen on it; he was; but it was too heavy. After much fruitless striving he sees an alert-looking pedestrian coming along, and tells him of his need. "Oh," says the stranger, "stick to it, you will do it all right; stick your feet in so, put your hands so, and never give up." Now clearly this advice might be excellent, but it would be perfectly useless by itself; inasmuch as the man knew before what to do, but was unable to do it. The spirit was willing, but the flesh....Well, after this hope was quenched, our friend saw another stranger coming along, obviously a man of colossal strength, who accosts him with the inevitable question, and then shows him how easily he, the stranger, can lift the stone. He replaces it and walks on.

The first man, clearly, is worse off than before. His difficulty is no less, but he has been shown that it is not recognized by others; and you note that if the exhortation had been ideal and combined with strength in the same person then the two together would have been still quite useless.

Therefore face squarely the alternative. Either take the Apostles' Creed as true, and be clear-headed enough to see that everything must give way to the paramount obligation of teaching it as *living* facts to the young, or drop it altogether and make the best of moral exhortation. But, for the sake of your own peace of mind and integrity of soul, avoid the pestilent heresy of supposing that if it is true no great harm will come of ignoring it; or that if it is not true some good will come of teaching it.

Too long to quote, but suggestive, is an analysis by Liszt of Chopin's temperament; so egoistic that for anyone who did not think exactly as he did and see life with his eyes he nourished a cold disdain. Notice how this bears on the need of selflessness we were discussing a week or two ago. You used to be fond of music. Did you ever thoroughly love Chopin's work?

Yours ever,

J.

Letter XXIX

Dear J.

In days when I had time to listen to piano playing I rarely felt quite at home with Chopin; and should have been sorry to see my daughter getting to be devoted to him. It is an interesting instance, but of course millions of others might be produced.

You are hard on the many fathers and schoolmasters who forgo religious teaching from a kind of despair. There is so much crazy controversy about it, and it is so easy to infect a youngster with downright horror of it that you can hardly wonder at many fighting shy. But I should agree cordially that, if true, Christianity must be all important; therefore, must be taught; further, that there must be at least one right way and probably many wrong ways of teaching it, and that there is no evidence to show that most of our parents and teachers have hit upon the right method or anything near it. Indeed one of the excuses for our pitiful vacillation and cold-heartedness is the apparent unwillingness of children to learn what is called the truths of Revelation. Our Creator gives them a heart that is astoundingly unreceptive. We are bidden to be like little children. Well, look at the results of all our efforts to teach them! Some 90 per cent. of the young men of England almost wholly ignorant, ready to identify Christianity with Moslemism! Does not that by itself give a warrant for our scepticism? Granted that He is all wise and all loving; and that there may be some reason for this kind of religious stupidity which we can't yet understand; yet the inference a plain man is bound to draw is that the truths which He, our Creator, has revealed are uncongenial to children, that is, the vast majority of them. Hence the best thing we can do is to present the Creed to them so that those who are drawn to it will apprehend it. As to the others, one must trust to example and moral training. I grant you they are proved ineffective and perhaps increasingly so, but what else is to be done? After all, the influence of a Christian atmosphere must tell, and if it were to die away no doubt the decay of morality would be deplorable. So we must peg away in our English, illogical fashion and hope for the best.

In short, I see that your reasoning points towards the over-whelming claim of education on our attention. I am with you in distrusting the effect of all this social work, so superficial, so confused, and ill-directed. It is becoming plain that we need a great guiding principle, one that can be understood by the young and that will commend itself generally to the adult male teacher. It is evident that we have not yet found it. Meantime it is better that morals without foundation should be taught, rather than that much time should be spent on principles which cannot be learnt. For in a mass of cases the result is nil, and we anyhow do some good by attacking symptoms of evil, if we can't agree about causes. Better, I mean, do the best we can to "muddle along" in teaching conduct with fair success, than quarrel about religion, which brings no success at all. That means, of course, the religious teaching will be rather pale, and perhaps a little overcautious lest it makes too much of a stir and provokes a controversy. But for practical people in a busy age is there anything else to be done?

Yours ever,

HENRY.

Letter XXX

Well, dear friend, you have treated me to an interesting letter and no mistake. I would that I could touch on all the questions you start. Do you remember Mat. Arnold's description of F. D. Maurice's writing: "He is always, and with the utmost emotion, beating about the bush but never starts the hare." Very graphic. But you do the opposite; you restrain the emotion lest it should be wasted, but from the bush many promising quadrupeds start, and I am fain to run after each singly, but like the poor bulls in the arena at Madrid, when they chase the foot-men, I should end by catching none.

Henry, when Sophocles said that man was the most wonderful thing in the Universe, was he not forecasting the modern Englishman? He gazed with astonishment at his contemporaries' achievements, the tillage of the land, seamanship, and the building up of the State. But how trivial is all this, and even all of our superadded inventions compared with the mysterious power an ordinary English Christian shows from day to day; of deeply believing and stoutly professing great imperishable principles of conduct, and then in his professional life, his surroundings, his talk, his walk, his dress, his plans, his pleasures and even in his conceit, his cruelty, his sorrows, flatly and complacently contradicting all that he knows to be true within him and without! Why didn't the singer of Colonus touch on this subversion of life? Because the Athenian had little perception of God's moral claims compared to our own aspirations, but what light he descried he followed in a singular boyish loyalty of spirit, pressing on through Art and Science to the outskirts of the Divine. Child-like in many respects; yes, but where is the child in us now? We have the knowledge of God, we own Him as our Creator, and stubbornly turn our backs upon Him; not in open defiance, for we are not clear-headed or honest enough to be rebels; but stiffly repudiating His foundation commands and building up all the damnabilities of our industrial system, laying the train for another world-wide war, without a suspicion of what we are doing!

But what am *I* doing, running on thus. Yet there is a coherence in my rhodomontade. If there has been a Revelation of God Himself must it not be so vitally necessary for us that it needs to be taught irrespective of results? From its essential majesty we might infer the paramount duty of teaching truth, but that our habit of ignoring our deepest convictions has blinded our eyes.

If I am right, the question of home training of children assumes new and immense proportions and may not be put by. What think you of this?

Yours ever,
JAMES.

Letter XXXI

Dear James,

I see that your last letter was an answer to my plea for results, and though I shall always find it very difficult to apply your doctrine I cannot gainsay it. Anyone who believes that God has spoken to mankind, entrusting truth to a few that they might pass it on, must be a lunatic if he does not hold the obligation to teach in greater reverence than any other practical duty whatever.

But look at the condition. Suppose we cannot bring ourselves to this belief. I mix with many high-minded men whose ideals are your ideals, whose whole life is lit with a lofty hope; but they would hesitate to say they are sure there has been any utterance from God distinct enough for us to build on. Their sense of the divine is vague compared to yours. Some of them find the highest thing in life through the teaching of Science; others in beauty, and a great many in social activities hoping to better the plight of their countrymen.

Now to them, and till recently I was one of them myself, there is something that smacks of arrogance in the positiveness of the claim to truth as you have put it. You will allow that no one can be expected to be a good listener or a good expositor of doctrines about which he is somewhat doubtful. Where he fails is of course just at the point where the doctrine is ready packed for transmission. Perhaps he loves it; but if so it is as a coloured mist floating round his path; but who can transmit a mist, or compress it into a parcel, or cabin it in a catechism? Δάκνει τόδ' ἤδη, I used to read. Here is where the most carefully made shoe continues to pinch.

Yours ever,
H.

Letter XXXII

Dear H.

You are doubtless right in thinking that many people flatter themselves they don't know what truth is, and are "driven about by every blast of vain doctrine." But I am concerned with those who do know and won't obey her. There are swarms of such on every side. Often their knowledge is half unconscious and sadly blurred. But deep down they grip the true thing and often acknowledge it—but can't or won't apply it. The tragedy of Pilate when he said "What is truth?" was that he knew all the time, and to his knowledge Christ was appealing. I mean he knew enough truth to act, and that is probably all that any of us know; anyhow till we have acted.

Everybody begins life with a very little faculty of perception, given in infancy, of a law higher than inclination. The whole drama of each soul turns upon whether he acts on that knowledge or ignores it. If he ignores it, it lingers in the mind as a sort of luminous vapour, not nearly so useful as fog; and Virgil's description of somebody becomes true of the middle-aged man, *Infert se saeptus nebula?*

The conviction of the truth of Christ's teaching is widespread —astonishingly so—especially of that which goes contrary to the current opinion. Witness what I reminded you of about the Tommies' facing of suffering, and our admiration of them. Again, if it were not so, how could Christianity have survived? We have done what we could to kill it, but it is imperishable, because everybody knows it to be true.

Well, is not this the position in Christendom, at least in western Europe? You have a swarm of highly civilized people who dislike thinking and believe in action, or anyhow give themselves to it unstintedly, and judge each other by the industry, the energy they put forth towards the one grand object of life, viz. acquisition; that being according to common consent the means of making the world a happier place. For centuries all the wisest men in every nation have preached that this way of bettering the world is doomed to failure, just because no amount of gain satisfies the hunger of the human soul; secondly, because there is not enough to go round. Thirdly, because if there were we have not yet gone near to learning how to distribute it. Viewed solely as a method of living for a few years on this planet, it is obvious that modern civilization is not so much civilized heathenism, but rather a jostling race of blindfolded multitudes—the foremost nations of the world—towards the same abyss.

Mark what I am saying. Competition as we conceive and practise it between classes or countries, merely from the point of view of a prudent man, is patently and undeniably turning earth into a hell. Mind, I daresay there are plenty of people who would say that they like it. I daresay they do, but that does not make it any the less hell. Hinton surely is right in saying that damnation is preferring selfishness to self-sacrifice, and if the preference brings no pain with it, it will continue without end. Pain, agony, torture, brought on by long continued selfishness, are the beginnings of the cure.

But this by the way. Notice, I beg you, that while this mad racing to destruction continues, the mass of the peoples so engaged profess themselves to be followers of Christ; some of them believers in the mystic promise of His presence and His grace among us, powerful to save, and in the redemption of the world brought about by His death; others, a huge number, unable to grasp the mysterious, are all the more ardent votaries of His moral teaching and example. This means that there are millions who really recognize that the life of self-offering, of service, of unchecked devotion to something wholly different from material welfare of any kind, is the only true life. They know it, and over and over again they testify to the depths of their knowledge. But they contradict it in practice, with a self-complacency no mortal man can explain.

The bearing of this on our subject may now be pointed out. I am discussing the question whether truths of revelation are to be taught for their own sake, irrespective of their results, or only where man can perceive their utility. Before tackling the kernel of the matter, I wish to insist that we are nearly all incapacitated for judging fairly of the vital importance of God's revelation, by the fact that we so flagrantly, persistently and blindly disavow our deepest and most sacred convictions in the much simpler sphere of morals. Consider: how can a poor fellow, who, for years on end, has unwittingly wrenched his mind away from God to self, be a judge of the awful mysteries committed to our faith and understanding, especially as he is bound to estimate them by the fatuous test of whether they are likely to help him and others in the struggle for material gain, or the gratifying of some peacock vanity and lust for applause.

Now, Henry, if this is true, education is one thing; if it is false, education is another thing. In the one case something simple, intelligible and lit up with a most radiant hope; in the other case, it is a sorry, tangled and worthless chaos of overlapping aims and endlessly abortive effort which at the start promises something, but never endures; and the more it is persisted in the more it withers away, sterile and redolent of death.

But steady. Is all this buncombe or not?

Yours ever,

JAMES.

Letter XXXIII

Dear J.,

"Buncombe" your letter emphatically was not. The maxim that, for Christians who believe in revelation, revealed truth must, for its own sake, be paramount, is unassailable, and should be a steadying principle for all who are concerned with education. When I ask myself next how are we to determine what truth is revealed, I am reminded of what you said as to the doing of God's Will being necessary to the knowledge of the doctrine. Now, practically, does that mean that every humdrum duty-doing clerk, or cattle-rancher, or politician is on his way to knowing all about God's doctrine? For if so, they are either a long way off reaching it, or else doctrine means something very different from what we hear in pulpits or in controversy, or I am still baffled by the phenomenon of the transparently honest self-less character who scarcely professes to be a Christian. If such characters can be trained you won't get the modern Englishman to bother his head about doctrine. Everybody is talking more volubly than ever of the need of "character-training" till one tires of the word. How it is to be done nobody knows. I am "bored stiff" by the noise made since 1914 by all sorts of chatter about re-modelling society, and a new spirit and the like, which is received with suspicious cordiality by congress audiences and indeed all gatherings of earnest citizens, dwindling though they appear to be in number. What we need is to see the connexion between this "new spirit" and ordinary religious teaching: for, frankly, it is a staggerer to find that the output of the Church schools is a young man not only no better behaved than that of the C.C. schools, but every whit as ignorant. You can't wonder at the general hesitation. It is horribly difficult to agree upon a common form of instruction; more difficult still to teach it effectively, and for the boys and girls apparently impossible to learn and therefore quite impossible to practise. On the whole I am astonished at the toleration shown to the Church-people. The Church insists as you do that truth must be taught for its own sake and then fails to teach it, and fails also to a large extent to agree as to what is to be taught. You will admit, I am sure, that this is a perplexing state of things; and though perplexity may be a necessary stage in the quest for truth, it is not one to rest in. But how to emerge, I know not.

I look with much eagerness to your next; though possibly some of my anticipation of its contents will not be wholly wrong.

Yours gratefully and expectantly,

HENRY.

Letter XXXIV

Well, my dear friend, the trail is getting warm, and you and I are "hot," as the children used to say. Suppose we make a vigorous effort to apply the principle of Truth to be taught for its own sake; we can afford to wait serenely for the good *results* to come. But your trouble is not so much about the results of successful teaching but about the huge proportion of failure.

Now need we be discomfited by finding Christian truth difficult to teach, and many of our efforts abortive? To begin with, who are the teachers? Why, all adults, in a measure. How many of the adults fulfil the condition that if their teaching is to be effective it must be backed up and commended by practice?

We have already agreed that though the true life is to be full of venturesomeness and the warrior spirit in the age-long combat with evil; though, again, the concomitant of this true life is an expansion and renewing of the personality; nevertheless its central and inviolable principle is a subordination of all natural inclination to a higher law; a stern refusal to allow the quest for anything the world calls desirable, in any circumstances whatever, to dominate the practice or determine the main aspirations of individuals or nations.

Now there is no dispute about the fact that this ideal of life is frankly, or with concealment, discarded by the vast majority of mankind. Nobody whose opinion is worth twopence can contemplate this state of things without dismay. We may buoy up our minds by telling each other of the greatness of God's Redemption of the World, and how that in some unthinkable way the Almighty will complete His scheme of Salvation. But meantime it is clear that we are bound to know anguish of heart at the obstinate perversity of our Father's children. Christ was a Man of Sorrows, and this was the reason.

So even men of no religious emotion admit that Christianity has never been fairly tried, and that the world would be the better if it were. So we believe we have found the panacea, and after a good deal of railing at the Church for being so impotent we form our committees, scrape together some thousands of pounds—nothing like enough—and set to work. Nothing happens, except that a lot of new social machinery has been set up and is with much groaning and fuss kept going. After many months of abortive effort mutual recrimination begins afresh.

Now, Henry, I affirm that real true encouragement comes when we first perceive that this *débacle* is not only other people's fault but our own (study, I beg you, Ps. lxxvii. 10, with context) and the fault has been not of slackness, nor of covetousness, nor of the sectarian temper—though there has been enough and to spare of all three; but of blindness born of dislike of God. We have failed to see the conditions under which alone we can hope. They are these: we must recognize the horrors of life as guides to right conduct; they are slime pits which mark the Broad Way and dispose us to turn and try the Narrow Way; not simply shocking things, calling for wringing of hands and mournful babblement at five o'clock teatime. But they are what they are only to believers in God, and that because He is set not on making things pleasant here, but on training our characters for the hereafter. So much of belief in Him is absolutely essential to anything we can dare to call reform or reconstruction.

One more point which will strike you as paradoxical now, but later I am sure you will concede it. We ought to choose our line of action not according to the success we can reckon on but by the reasonableness of the hope which is suggested: that is to say, where the need is most acute and the remedy most natural, there is a strong presumption that there is the quarter to which we should press. Apply that principle to the matter in hand. The civilized nations are set on the wrong thing, and there is no hope of a change unless a new spirit can be planted. That is simply to say that the best hope by far lies in the children, and hence the conclusion is perfectly plain that everything that is possible should be done to restore what was sound in the training of the English home of fifty years ago, and quicken it.

But enough. The practical outcome of this bristles with difficulties, but so far *hast du etwas dagegen?* As R. B. remarks in the *Lost Leader*, " Life's night begins," or as Jebb renders it, *Pergimus in tenebras.*

Yours ever,

J.

Letter XXXV

My dear James,

At times I feel rather like those who listened to Artemus Ward's lecture on the Dark Races. But anon the "golden gates appear." Now I began by looking up the verse in Ps. lxxvii and discovered what you meant by the encouragement of realizing one's own blunder of understanding as well as weakness of will. There is something paralyzing about our early recognitions of the latter; we quail before the repeated evidence of infirmity so radical, so incurable. At that stage, then, nothing could be more cheering than to discern that after all we have been guilty of crass stupidity as well as of rebellion against God; that the old saying about thoughtlessness being productive of more misery than crime is, after all, perfectly true, and thoughtlessness is less inaccessible as a disorder than the deliberate preference of evil to good.

Then on looking back on your letters I made out what you meant by the two incompatible aims which are designated by the words God and Mammon; and that the second of these is not the selfish ignoring of our neighbours' claims, but the mad attempt to construe as self-sacrifice what is really self-gratification. Or in other words, we persuade ourselves that to ensure first our own comfort in life and give the residue of our thought and energy to helping others, is the same as seeking *first* the Kingdom of God, when in reality it is the exact opposite.

If I am right the malady is largely intellectual and therefore more patient of treatment than if it were only moral. It looks as if all the time a great number of people really want to do right; whereas many of our morally and spiritually gifted contemporaries have been talking as if mankind in the large preferred evil to good. I daresay some do; but it is a huge comfort to believe that the majority do not. Moreover, it is now plain to me how directly all this touches on education, for if men are blind as to the two roads, there is hope in teaching. If they are incurably weak, or incurably perverse in their choice, *il n'y a pas de moyen*.

But there is much in your letter which is obscure. Tell me, good counsellor, if I am right so far.

It sometimes comes across me that it would be difficult to find anyone to answer these questions, in Lombard Street or Belgravia no less than in Thibet or Terra del Fuego, but, I suppose, not impossible. But amid the general prevalence of blindness, how great is the power of the true vision; which, instead of being ignored, always compels attention! There is something about this quest which makes me less inclined to give ten hours a day to increasing my income. Not that business is wrong, but that something else is much more right.

Yours ever,
H.

Letter XXXVI

O demonish man! as Plato or Socrates used to call one who had hold of part of the truth but hesitated to press on, you have only to push steadily on from the point you have reached. There is something much more right than business. What? or Why? Why, service, to be sure, and in some cases business is service; and we have to ask what is the motive of service? for whatever else is sure this is, that we are born into this world with inclinations which pull against service in any shape, and make for manifold forms of ego-centricity; some of them most winsome and deceptive; some such as to stir misgiving or, at least, reflection. (Someone once said that walking down any London street you see many faces that "make you reflect." Would it were London only!)

But whisht! a not indispensable visitor is at the door, and I must stop before I had begun.

Yours,
J.

Letter XXXVII

Dear J.,

I forgot to thank you for reminding me of Jebb's trans-
lations. I take them down from the shelf at times and forget for
a brief spell "that dust and din and steam of town: Libo, Janus,
Marsyas." But I wish, O how I wish, that I had followed the
plan of a lady friend hard by who in her girlhood learnt to escape
from the chatter of callers or the rough and tumble of younger
brothers into the woods, where, like Brahms before breakfast,
she gathered nourishment from the foliage of common trees;
and now, when vexed by an onset of life's small disquietudes,
she escapes to an upper chamber and gives herself to a picture
book of her forest favourites which bring back to her some calm
of spirit; some memories of fellowship with the noiseless pulsa-
tions of our mighty Mother's unwearied life, till the fretful
claims of modern Chelsea assume their right proportion, and the
self is laid to rest again. There, by the way, is something to think
of in home or perhaps school training, for she was in her teens
when she first learnt the secret spell of green leaves and curving,
curly, branches.

You have brought my debilitated feet to a slippery slope in
the upward path and they keep on reversing the motion required.
Odd that it comes to the same want of progress if the surface be
slippery or sticky! But all indications go to show that it is an
effort uphill, which is, after all, encouraging. The only easy
movement is in the wrong direction. I mean that as soon as you
pass from morality to the fact of God's Presence, to religion, in
short, I at once am pulled up short by a sensation of the arduous;
and the mental muscles begin to protest, yearning like the Irish-
man after the flat surface again. That worthy, you remember,
was found on a day's journey in a very hilly country walking
backwards and forwards on a flat 10 yards and explaining:
"Bedad, when I get a level bit, I must make the best of it."

Morality I can understand; but religion? You imply that
everything depends on sincere belief. I should only agree there
if you are using the idea of God far more widely than is usual.
Compared to your handling of this most august theme, the popular idea of God is at once strangely vague and strangely narrow;

qualities which one would think were hardly compatible. The Name suggests something limitlessly vast, but in action anyhow most restricted and curiously inoperative. As soon then as you enter on this lofty theme, I feel as if "we were the first that ever burst into that silent sea."

Moreover, if you are right in postulating that moral training should be supplemented by religion, how do you explain the beggarly results of strict religious training? Is it not a fact that there is nothing really to choose either as to conduct or knowledge even between the output of Church and County Council schools? I have a vague recollection of a controversy over statistics when some Bishop was challenged for evidence of superior character-training being the result of Church teaching as compared with that of Board schools—some twenty years ago—and he failed egregiously to produce it. One would have thought this sort of fact would have dished the whole system of doctrinal teaching or indeed of religious teaching in general; but lo! the House of Commons has never given in to the demand for secular teaching in all schools. Why not? Was ever hugger-mugger more complete than this?

Your reasoning seems solid against more moral training; but when it is supplemented by the best religious teaching that can be given nothing seems to happen. Where are we now?

Yours ever,

HENRY.

Letter XXXVIII

My dear H.,

You have put your finger on a singular symptom of British psychology, and not for the first time have we come upon it. To all appearances your Briton is a convinced believer in the maxim about the proof of the pudding being in the eating. He repeats it and you almost catch him in the act of practising it by destroying the Church schools; at least he makes it into an excuse for stopping his subscriptions. But when asked to vote for secularization of teaching, not he! It has been a similar story I find about the public schools.

A youth not long ago wrote an indictment—*fanda nefanda*; especially the latter—against these venerable and peculiarly British institutions. Judging from the way the book was read, and the scanty criticism it received, you would say it was believed far and wide. Indeed I met several thoughtful men who declared it must be true in the main. Yet my schoolmaster cousin tells me that since that book was published and read the schools have been fuller than ever! How do you explain this sort of thing? There is only one thing to be said. The British mind is fortified by sound convictions which lie too deep to be uttered but have again and again saved the country from plunging into the quagmire of heedless experiment and will o' the wisp undertakings. John Doe and Dick Roe are not to be judged by what they profess. If our political action were to be rated by our political talk we should occupy a foremost place among the charlatans of mankind. Our spoken principles are laughable stuff indeed; but we have done many wise things quite unwittingly, sometimes while actually telling each other we were doing the opposite. Then we have been saved from fatal self-congratulation by inability, even after the achievement, to understand what has happened. Not only did we "build up the British Empire in a fit of absence of mind"—I heard John Seeley utter those pregnant words on the platform in 1880—but we had no notion, till Parkin and Chamberlain told us, what it was we had done. Thus we were saved from self-complacency by our native blindness; but to-day there is serious risk that our modern efforts to probe the situation will induce the "swelled head." Serious, because though you may build up unobserved a Church, a State and an Empire, when your head begins to swell other people are bound to know it. Thus foreigners have observed that we make our revolutions without bloodshed. That is because we have no idea what we are doing; and it is easy to abstain from slaughter when you don't think that anything particular is going on.

Now this deep and undisturbed stratum of conviction is a gift of Nature which may be destroyed by our perceiving it, analyzing it, and then pluming ourselves upon it; but which is fairly safe still, as long as 90 per cent. of our people are unaware of its existence. In regard to religion, however, it is exposed to the dangers of non-recognition, such as lack of buoyancy and hope, and failure to take effect in corporate action. For corporately we talk nonsense, except when we are, as often, possessed by a dumb devil.

Therefore let us never be staggered when we come upon the weirdest inconsistencies in our history. What we are up against at the present moment is a strange resolve to continue our religious teaching, though, as regards both learning and conduct, we admit that we have failed. This you have noted. It must be because we still have a hold upon the divine. The Englishman at birth enters upon a noble heritage of readiness to learn about God and to understand good music. His "feet are set in a large room," but we have nearly killed the first with bad teaching and the second with no teaching at all. "Bad teaching"—of what sort? Again I must ask you to weigh well what I say at this point.

Much fuss and some fun have been made over the technical blunders of our religious lesson, our prosing "about Huppim, Muppim and Ard," or the exact distance between Joppa and Mahanaim. The less obtuse among us have laughed at this woeful failure to distinguish between a dull Scripture lesson and the glorious thing that has always been a possibility for the opening of a young soul to the influence of the Holy Spirit Himself.

The failure has been made inevitable by our allowing free play to a counteracting influence of overwhelming power. Do you see what I mean? I will not explain further for the present— *alio enim debemur.*

Yours always,

JAMES.

Letter XXXIX

Well, James, I never. There is something comic in your puzzling me with a question which I can hardly understand. I think, however, you have diagnosed the national mind with some skill, and that may lead me to a discovery.

The "counteracting influence" to our religious teaching? Well, of course, I know little of the inside of schools, but, looking back on my own boyhood, I can see now that the religious teaching was very feeble—dull and often quite dead—but isn't it always so? Some of the masters were quite interesting on other subjects, but I can't remember that the Bible lessons ever gripped life as we knew it; though some of the sermons in chapel did. Or do you mean the games were made too much of? I hope not; people are saying they are the cause of our men fighting so well, and I should be surprised if there is not an ebullition of athleticism when peace comes. Undoubtedly a lot of young fellows are turned out into the world content to lead rather selfish lives, but I suppose it always has been so; and after all they certainly work harder and are more chaste than fifty years ago.

But in all this there is nothing to be called a "counteracting influence," at least not by one who chooses his words with anything like precision. So I am, not for the first time, baffled, but expectant. We keep on pouncing, or being about to pounce rather, on something so central to education that though I have blown away many cobwebs from my brain I have not felt ready to begin any practical work with my offspring.

By the way you can't mean—can you?—that the obstacle for girls is their school life or the opening of careers for them?

Yours ever,
H.

Letter XL

Dear H.,

I think I may say that if you see eye to eye with me about this "obstacle" we shall be at one on the whole of the questions you have raised. Sooner or later, I mean. This hope fillips me up smartly.

To what do certain facts we have noted point? They are (1) that the religion taught to all of us, claims to be a message of joy, but practically is judged by most of us to be gloomy; (2) that the claim of Christianity is for unstinted self-sacrifice, whereas nearly all Christians only go as far as is convenient; (3) that the Bible teaches a view of suffering which is directly opposed to the fashionable view of to-day in every European country, but ratified by our homage when we see it practised; (4) that religion fails to achieve any of the improvements of society which have been hoped for, and yet the country cannot make up its mind to give it up. They point to this much: that Christianity as presented in this country is a gloomy religion, and therefore ineffective, especially among the young; though there seems to be something of a predisposition in the hearts of the people to respect and love it when it is put into practice.

Thousands of earnest people, deploring the ineffectiveness, put it down to the gloom of the teaching, and are clamouring successfully for "brighter" services. But where the bright services are tried, though a temporary stir is made ineffectiveness resumes its dismal reign.

Now beyond any doubt whatever, Christianity has been widely taught in a form terribly unlike that presented by its Founder. That has been to some extent corrected, yet still the results are extremely poor. Let us ask ourselves if some fundamental condition of the Gospel message being accepted has not been violated? Let us ignore for the nonce the manifold defects of the teachers and consider if there is not some obstacle in the minds of the taught which makes it difficult for them to receive the Gospel.

I don't suppose you, after all you have written, will dispute this diagnosis of the situation. Christ—the supreme Author and Authority of all good living—has laid it down as impossible for a human being to aim at pleasing himself and at the same time to an equal degree pleasing God. One must be first. (We may infer in passing that whenever man tries to put the two on an equality he is putting Mammon first, though he may not know it.) What then is likely to be the effect of this paramount fundamental law being set at nought? What, I mean, will be man's receptivity of divine truth if he disobeys the law laid down?

To answer that crucial question we must remark that what Christ taught was primarily a certain view of things, or interpretation of life; secondarily, *as an expression of this interpretation*, a certain kind of conduct. He never enjoined the conduct as good or beneficial or desirable for its own sake, or for any reason whatever except as a corollary of the interpretation.

The interpretation, crudely worded, was that man is created by a Father who loves him, and desires above all things that the love should be returned, and deals with His creatures always with the purpose of evoking love. When we recognize that purpose we begin to see that life is not a chaos but a glorious harmony. No sooner is that realized than our thoughts and feelings are changed in three directions more and more day by day: towards God, towards our neighbour, towards ourselves. Towards God they become all gratitude, towards other men all service, towards ourselves they die away; mortified, because that on which we are inclined to feed them is seen to be nothing.

Now very soon we shall have to consider how these eternal principles can be passed on to others as a living and most precious treasure which is not lessened for *A* when he gives it to *B*.

So let me know just where you stand. Dear me! just to think of us middle-aged pilgrims between the cradle and the grave wrestling with these primeval problems, as if for the first time! How unlike what we used to talk of on our walking tours in those long-past Easter holidays! Do you remember the sunlight playing on Kynance Cove? and the first April wheat-ear that showed he was not really afraid of man? "Canty days, John," but there are better!

Ever yours,

J.

Letter XLI

ANSWER: Excuse p.c.; push on, I beg. Is it *pueriliter pueros* to talk much of pain beforehand? Would it not be deterrent?

H.

Letter XLII

Dear Henry,

I am not recommending much talk about anything. A parent "full of words shall not prosper on the earth." But the joy of pain can be learnt by living it. For take note that if we obey our best and truest instincts we commit ourselves to a life of self-sacrifice or love which is the forgetfulness, the disowning of self. This is, I fancy, the law which Jesus promised to fulfil, and this is the blessedness which comes by not being sought.

I assume you go with me in the matter of the grand obstacle to true living in these times. Doubtless it has been the same in all ages. If children are allowed to grow up with their native conviction undisturbed that they are in this world *primarily* to "have a good time" it is impossible they can be followers of Christ. To this conclusion His best known words and all His example bind us down.

Recognizing this, we cast about for every variety of compromise, and especially in our education. We set before our boys —and nowadays our girls too—a prospect of a well-equipped happy active life as the thing to be desired and as far as possible secured. This programme is entirely congenial to the child, with one considerable modification. Many a child exhibits propensities which if not checked will bring him into collision with the world: such as rampant greediness, likely to develop later into breaches of the seventh and eighth Commandments. Any prudent mother puts her foot down here. She makes it clear to Tommy that in some respects he must bridle his appetites or he will find the indulgence of them not worth the cost. But, note carefully, this amount of discipline—though far more than is often exercised—leaves the native egoism undisturbed, or rather, corroborated, since effort involved in striving for a prize generally enhances its value, "and of course my parents know." So for egoistic reasons he checks the ego here and there. Now another boy that is not greedy but self-complacent and cold, a possible Pharisee of the English complexion, is very attractive often during boyhood, but steadfastly and always set on making life what he would like it to be. He is not what people call self-indulgent, but successful in a "good" sense of the word; just such a result as really sensible citizens of weight and repute will always approve, look for and assist. It will perhaps be a refined life, adequately though not sumptuously furnished with the defences against suffering and loss which the world offers so glozingly to each rising generation, such as friends, income, leisure, and interesting work, and which nearly every one of us has to find out to be more or less of a mirage in life's arid sand, though in prospect "so wondrous sweet and fair."

How, Henry, let us jointly make a violent effort to keep to the point. I would have you note that we are called upon to estimate, not the known and admitted shortcomings in our education, but the *aim and intention of it at its best.* A community, like an individual, is to be judged less by what it achieves than by what it hopes and desires.

This large object of desire then, this fairly ample and fairly equipped life is set before every youngster in nearly all "good" homes as the ideal. There can be no two opinions as to its attractiveness. Even after disillusionment the adult hankers after it or clings to its residuum. How immensely potent then must it be to the young! But let it be as attractive as words can picture it, is it true? Does it present life to the youngster as life really is?

There, my sagacious comrade in life's journey, is the central question for every one of us; central, because wriggle as we may we must face it, and as a plain matter of fact we must and do answer it, and on the answer everything depends. There we are. Now tell me if you go with me to this point and let me know what you think must come next.

Yours,

JAMES.

Letter XLIII

My dear James,

I cannot deny that your picture corresponds with the facts. It presents the ideal towards which the whole civilized world is working, nay striving, plotting, fighting. Perhaps something more should be said about training in charity and social work; and you seem to imply that the teaching of religion has no very marked effect in modifying the main interpretation of life which our children are practically certain to imbibe from their parents, their environment generally, and the spirit of the times. But I would not suggest that these omissions detract from the truthfulness of the description of what is going on in the homes and schools of the foremost peoples of to-day.

Is it all wrong? and if so, why?

I can see that you are going on to say it is all wrong. But if you do, won't you be a *vox clamantis in deserto?* Perhaps you won't object to that rôle after all. It certainly has a noble tradition behind it. But an interesting comment on your letter has been given me in the nick of time by young Canon Hopley, who dropped in here owing to trouble with his push-bike yesterday;

and though I know him only slightly he struck me as likely to be keenly interested in our investigations. So I showed him your screed: and wrote down what he said before it "evaded" from my leaking *cerebellum*.

"There are two rather obvious criticisms to make on the modern ideal of training the young, which I conceive your friend has very correctly diagnosed. (1) It plainly traverses the main principles of conduct and living laid down by Christ. (2) Less plainly but still apparently it has failed practically. If very nearly all the foremost members of the successful nations pursue their quest with unanimous ardour, we certainly want some explanation of the present chaotic condition of the world. If the ideal has failed it cannot be because it has been half-heartedly sought. Perhaps it is due to economic causes, that the good things of the world won't go round, or that they would if we knew how to distribute them; in short, that a state of happiness of the minority demands servitude of the majority, and that the time for that is past for ever. I consider both criticisms unanswerable but unconvincing. If this ideal of life is sound, then the mere authority of the Gospel will not destroy it. The second criticism merely means that when we have learnt how to adjust social conditions the thing will work; it is question of time. My conviction, however, is that the ideal can be, and ought to be, attacked for some more unassailable reason than either of these, but I am not prepared at the moment to say what it is."

This anyhow may give you a starting point for your next. It is strange to find a Canon dissatisfied with the indictment that a certain teaching is unchristian, and apparently wanting something stronger!

Yours ever,

Henry.

Letter XLIV

My dear Henry,

I should like to shake hands with that young Canon; a man of discernment I must reckon him. Why, he has saved me two long letters. It is only necessary now to follow his lead in the matter of the Gospel.

See where we are. The mass of society—all classes and all ages and both sexes—pursues an ideal of life which is congenial to their inclinations, and varies according as those inclinations have been guided into a conventionally "good" channel, or have been left to run riot. The outcome is most disquieting. Are we to try for something else? say, the ideal of cross-bearing?

Now, if so, I agree cordially with the Canon that it must not be simply because Christ orders it. If we were better children of the Most High that would be enough. We should long ago have discovered that the life He led *is, not was, the true life*. As it is we are not quite sure. So God implants in all of us a deep and wonderful instinct for recognizing that in spite of a thousand objections the cross-bearing ideal is the right one. Hence, I hold that we may commend it to each other, not baldly, because it is in the Gospel; but because "the light that is within us" shows us its supreme worth, and that it is a good plan first to consider it from the side of experience and our own deeper intuitions, then to compare notes with the Bible and find our notions corroborated and translated there into glorious action for our illumination and example.

Also the Canon is right in distrusting the economic argument, not only because it is disputable—everything is that, seemingly —but because it leaves the egoistic motive untouched. Indeed it does worse, it appeals to it with a prudent, middle-aged, Cheapside sagacity, saying "Of course you are right in hoping and scheming to gratify your desires; the refined, well-equipped, unsuffering life is within your reach, only you must change your tack. Recognize that the working-classes are beginning to insist on more refinement, etc., in their own lives; we can't gainsay them, but how the demand is to be met is another matter. Only let there be no paltering with the grand object you have set before yourself. Stick to what you have got as long as with any show of reason and patriotism you can do so. If you have to relinquish these things—*linquenda tellus et domus et placens uxor* —well, make the best of it, something will turn up. Anyhow it is of no use fighting against the whole mass of contemporary opinion. Renunciation is of course to be postponed as long as possible, but when it becomes inevitable we can lump it. There is nothing else to be done."

At this point may we not say there is in theory no disagreement except as to the *degree* of self-renunciation or self-giving, as I prefer to call it, which is to be taught? From every quarter of the globe comes a call for a new spirit of brotherliness and unselfishness. Yes, but is not that a plain proof that the ideal of the refined life of comfort (as I call it for short) has been found wanting?

Suppose the opposite were true: viz. that all that is required is for the pursuit of the comfortable ideal to be more thoroughly undertaken, more unanimously taught than it is, could any sane man call that a *new* spirit? It would be the old spirit, only more of it. Besides, the civilized world, instead of being faced with ruin and self-annihilation and every conceivable horror, would be actually in process of amendment, for the pursuit of comfort is far more general than it was prior to 1800, and that is true of all the leading nations. Yet everybody who has the slightest right to speak, insists that unless this new spirit *displaces* the old we are all hurrying pell-mell into the gulf of self-destruction and mutual slaughter.

Now I think I can forecast an objection from your side. Let me have it by return, as I am eager to press on.

Yours as ever,

JAMES.

Letter XLV

Dear friend,

A possible objection would be that you have over-stated the case. But that seems to me doubtful—very. When I hear of governments ordering the invention of the most damnable gases to wipe out whole multitudes of human beings in half a minute, and can certify that it is so, I fail to see that exaggeration is any longer possible. No; but there is a deeper difficulty.

Granted that unless the new spirit displaces the old one we are done for, and that the old one was the worship of material or temporary goods, is not your panacea the old spirit in a new dress? It looks like another and more sagacious attempt to make life pleasant, on the basis of mutual corporate action, because competition and national selfishness have broken down. Apart from its difficulties, is there not something fundamentally poisonous in the principle?

Yours ever,

HENRY.

Letter XLVI

My dear Henry,

Just what I expected. Now, dear man, note very carefully what I say.

There would be no possible answer to the objection you have put, unless from the strong, invariable, assumption of a God running this world as a training ground of character. I believe you would assent to that, and in fact all thoughtful Christians I find seem to agree. But the next point is more difficult. It is that an essential part of that training always has been according to the law of faith, by which I mean man has to be schooled to obey when he cannot see what good it will do, and there are very few of us mortals who do not kick when the demand is presented to us in this light.

Here, indeed, our religion comes in whether we wish it or not. Our life must be either Godward or worldly, the latter adjective being used as widely as possible, to include the most favourable, the best sort of worldliness. But before explaining that let me give the sense in which I use "Godward."

The unique thing about Christ was that He never for one moment appears to have aimed at happiness, either for Himself or for others. Yet He taught that by being renounced or merged into something infinitely higher, it was inevitably secured but in an unimaginably higher form. That is to say, by subjugating every desire to the paramount object of life, viz. the doing of God's will and so learning to love Him, the ideal of living may be attained, for in truth it is within everyone's reach. But it demands a certain interpretation of life which is not natural to man but yet can be taught and must be taught by His followers to others who know it not (Mt. iv. 17; xxviii. 19).

Now contrast with that the best sort of purely worldly ideal. Imagine a life wholly devoted to making others happy in the ordinary sense of the word. Even if the self-devotion means the very acme of self-abnegation, the most impressive, heroic self-lessness, the most winning blend of the virile and the tender, sympathetic, elements of character, it must of course be largely inspired and quickened by the Divine Spirit; but for the object of which you and I are in quest, it cannot be said to be the real thing. For it cannot be taught nor can its basic principle be made intelligible. To ignore so fair a work of His is to rebel against God. Moreover, it is open to the formidable indictment that, if unsuccessful, it is meaningless; whereas the Godward life thrives upon failure more than on success, and success in a world of growing complexity is becoming more and more remote. Indeed civilized mankind is faced by problems which are manifestly too intricate, too obstinate and too novel for the finest brains in the world.

What think you of this?

Yours ever,

J.

Letter XLVII

Candidly, James, and we are nothing if not candid—I don't yet feel comfortable about the "poison" objection which I put in my last. You see I am feeling after something very sublime and unassailably true, for it will have to be the *summum bonum* for my own children; the fair, august, glorious ideal of conduct to the striving for which I long for them to grow. So it must be beyond and above all taint of suspicion. Your contention reminds me unpleasingly of a comment made by a waggish friend on Balfour's *Foundations of Belief*, viz. that it was an appeal similar to that addressed by a shipwrecked man floating away from the wreck on a spar, to his mate: "Jack, I guess we had better begin to trust in Providence; for it looks as if there were nothing else to trust in." I want something free of all savour of second-best.

Yours ever,

H.

Letter XLVIII

Dear H.,

Your comment would remain, and we should have to shut up shop, if God were anything but what He is, or if His challenge to us came from a Being on the same level of life as ourselves. If God is what you and I believe Him to be, then clearly trust in Him must be the keynote of our character-training, no matter what results on our temporal prosperity and outlook it may seem to promise. Before Pentecost nobody could have understood this, but something happened then which made it possible.

Briefly, it comes to this. Our first thought when presented with a difficult job—too difficult I mean for our *cerebella*—is that we are not being fairly dealt with by our Creator. How inevitable that conclusion is if once we adopt the premises of the respectable lovable Englishman, that we are in the world to make it a place happy in the mundane sense! Do grip this firmly and be quite sure that you have done so before you have another quiet talk with Jack about anything, for on your doing so depends the question whether he learns from you what faith is, or has to pick it up elsewhere.

The other conclusion is as simple as can be. Granted that to learn to trust and love God is the object of life (Mt. xxii. 37), can we not rejoice in our being baffled by difficulties, clogged with our own infirmities, stupidities, greed; because the knowledge of our nothingness is a very prime condition of our trusting in Him. How grotesque the frame of mind of a County Councillor who on Sunday sings with emotion

> Nothing in my hand I bring,
> Simply to Thy Cross I cling,

and on Monday really persuades himself that his committees are going to lift the life of London; though every symptom goes to show that not one man in fifty has striven in prayer to God for guidance! Now don't let anyone tell you I am implying that man may be inert and God do the work. Not a bit of it. We have to "agonize" in practical work as well as in prayer, but the first without the second is a wretched farce and to its wretchedness all history testifies. So think, plot and devise an environment for Jack which shall make him conceive of an ideal for every effort much higher than any good the effort promises, and translate that ideal into words he can understand which will connect his hopes with God always. Never let yourself or him think of a difficulty except as a stimulus to trust, and, as such, a cause for thankfulness.

Similarly, what are you going to teach about life's failures?

Don't go the way of all genial optimistic maunderers in this subject. They try to get the youngster to believe that there is something wrong about failure. There may have been a wrong choice of policy and there generally is a wrong aim; but failure in a wrong aim, i.e. not God's will, is better than success. It all comes to the same point again. If the personality, power and love of God are apprehended, life's tumbles matter nothing, for if we do His will the failure can only be apparent.

In other words, the Godward life is lived in the growing conviction that out of our finite evils and horrors, infinite good comes, anyhow to those who understand the meaning of them. That meaning is understood by being taught, then by being seen, and then by being lived. That is the secret of all education, and our supreme obligation.

But the best mundane life has only one principle—a very noble one perhaps—which has hitherto failed and seems to fail more ignominiously the more persistently it is tried. It is to make the world happy and not think of God seriously except as a possible coadjutor in this emprize; and in that character it must be owned He is a most uncertain help, indeed He is no better than a Committee of the Cabinet. Between these two principles the choice must be made; and the first requisite is that the fundamental and irreconcilable difference between the two should be clearly recognized by all teachers of the young.

Yours ever,
JAMES.

Letter XLIX

Dear friend,

I have been pondering on your last, and what I come to is that there is nothing which the intellect can urge against your conclusion, because you base it ultimately on the infinite greatness of God, and further you fortify us beforehand in our undertakings by showing the meaning of failure and its hope. In contemplating the question of home training, then, we must recognize for our encouragement that the difficulties are in our languid will even more than in our obtuse understanding. Yet there is real encouragement in the fact, inasmuch as whatever is our own fault is remediable, and just now a whole lot of wise-acres are somehow taking on themselves to despair. Clearly if you are right they are wrong. I can pick no hole in your statement, but none the less the world at this moment cannot be described by the veriest Mark Tapley as a cheerful panorama, though I do find real comfort in your reminder that it is arranged to be an arena for the training of character. Perhaps that ought to be enough assurance for an ordinary father of ordinary children, and it would certainly give a noble background to the kind of home training we are in quest of, you and I.

Not objections or arguments or captious criticisms, but one or two questions remain, which you will allow your muddled-headed friend to put.

1. What is the attainable ideal in a modern home? I mean as to atmosphere and aspiration? I cannot quite picture the family life.

2. For instance, how should a boy be dealt with who betrays a real financial ability, and is certain to make a good thing of it if he goes into business? Is the career so compatible with Christian ethics and the life of service that he could be made to see that for him it is the true life, and that there need be no compromising with principle whatever?

3. You have said much about self-abnegation, self-repression, etc. Is such teaching possible for the rising generation who are dead set on "self-expression" and cannot brook anything that savours of repression? Has not the day for it passed, with the Feudal system, Mrs Grundy, and the belief in the serfdom of the working-men?

Yours gratefully,
Henry.

Letter L

My dear friend,

Whether your three questions vex you or not, there is no doubt they are in the air and provoke a vast amount of discussion. Let us see what is to be said about No. 1; the other two must wait.

You ask for something of a picture of a model home, not a superlative unearthly picture of impossible family life, but an outline which in spite of being nothing short of celestial is well within the reach and compass of any parents in the land. It has been my privilege to know one such.

A lady who went to stay in the house of a relative was taken ill there and obliged to remain for some weeks, during which she observed what was going on. The family consisted of two parents, astoundingly busy people, engaged in the service of God and of their fellowmen, all day and every day. There were, say, six children, three boys and three girls, between the ages of two and seventeen. Her first vivid impression was that of fun reigning in the household—clean, noisy fun. Her bedroom was over the diningroom, and as she lay there ill but noticing things, she heard through the floor almost continuous laughter! Occasionally a puckered-browed visitor would come to luncheon and play the part of a wet, or, rather, damp blanket for a season; but the moisture soon evaporated in that air, and though he was left curiously dry, he could no longer quench their mirthfulness.

A reaction, you will say, from strenuous working hours. Not at all; as the sick guest gradually learnt, it was a natural result of the view of life taken by everybody in the house, namely, that each was in the world to help somebody else every day, not as an annoying interruption to the serious business of amusement, but as the normal thing! This had come about not because the children were temperamentally pietistic or saintly or monkish or anaemic, but primarily because they noted that their parents, whom they loved and honoured, were engaged in beneficent activities from morning to night and never touched any recreation without sucking mental nourishment thereout. Originally the children were none of them remarkably endowed with cleverness or sparkle. Nor were they by nature docile and obedient, meek or conformable, but clamorous, self-assertive, noisy and sometimes annoying. Indeed our guest-witness testifies that if the home atmosphere had been different they might easily have grown up to be not the salt of the earth, as they each and all are by now, but an offence to heaven, and a nuisance to all their friends.

What then was it which produced such excellent results from quite ordinary material?

Certain facts were to be noted. I have said the mirth was

especially ebullient at mealtime. This was not because the food was a culinary triumph, rich or remarkably plentiful. It was always plain, and as a result less was eaten than in other houses, simply because when hunger was assuaged there was no inducement to go on eating.

That, however, though important, is a negative matter. Positively there is this to be said: from their earliest years the children have been accustomed to hear much talk and questioning about helping other people; always as the *best* thing that anyone could do, especially if it involved sacrifice of convenience or amusement. The deeply-rooted delusion, that we are justified in consulting our inclinations first, was extirpated by the elders taking for granted that it was not in anyone's thoughts. At breakfast, instead of projects for securing pleasure during the day, the young folk found themselves drawn into plans which had no meaning except service. Gradually all life was interpreted in terms of that object, and as the self sank more and more out of sight, the joy increased. But even the joy was not for a moment made the object of any endeavour. On the holidays all loafing, purposeless lounging and random journeyings were naturally taboo. Somehow, though no one was very artistically inclined, nourishment was always looked for in pictures, church architecture, and scenery, and though plenty of wholesome banter served to soften angles and promote fellowship, no such thing as drivelling talk was known. Hence they all found their greatest happiness in each other's company. Few more beautiful domesticities have ever been seen than the mutual affection that reigned quite undisturbed in this family circle.

Hence one serious difficulty was greatly mitigated. Instead of the standard of luxury, equipment for means of amusement, etc., being determined for them by a prodigal and self-indulgent set of neighbours, or by frequent visits to rich houses, made for no reason but in the hope of a "good time," this family dropped into a way of finding life really rewarding on a minimum of external resources. They were not allowed to take credit to themselves for this uncommon peculiarity, nor even to notice it. For the father's personality made this possible. The boys early learnt that he was earnestly set on their welfare and entered with zest into the innocent sports of their childhood. When, then, he said that the much coveted gewgaws of life, riding, expensive games, and any form of meaningless frolic were not to be, not another word was said. The children took it for granted that the prohibition was of the essence of wisdom: for was it not father's wish? Moreover they speedily learnt that happiness is not attained but rather forgone by overmuch provision for it. In short, it comes according as it is not longed for or pursued.

Connected with this was a very interesting feature of their family life. In days before the war, such a household was well supplied with servants; but the practice was for none of the children to rely on the offices of the domestics for their personal wants. The boys blacked their boots and their sisters' shoes, and any that were badly blacked had to be done again. The girls did most of the needlework for their brothers, and all made their own beds. Of course all out-door work to do with games was entirely done by the boys who learnt carpentering, painting and woodcraft of all sorts, dividing the labour according to their gifts, but no one of them dreamt of shirking his due share of the common toil; and so by the end of their school days the clumsiest-fingered of them was a fairly "handyman," and—far better than that—they all found relish in doing jobs for other people. A good average proficiency was secured by the simple rule that the full inconvenience and discomfort of any clumsy work were visited as far as possible on the workman.

It was noticeable too that when things went wrong the parents never found fault openly. What I have inferred was that the mother would always go into the matter enough to find out if anyone was to blame, and then in the gentlest way get the offender to see that through some small selfishness he, or she, had lost an opportunity of doing some active good, of giving something, and had made the blunder of supposing that there can be fruit gathered from egoism. But the moral lesson was seldom put into words. Events enforced it quietly and deeply. This was perhaps the only touch of genius in the handling of the children by the parents. What was distinctive in the training so far was the thoroughness with which principles admitted by everybody were practised.

But yet the deepest and greatest quality of this home has not yet been mentioned. Combined with a rare immunity from scolding, the children discovered, without being aware of it, that all duty was presented to them on a background of religion. That is to say, they never were led to suppose that the rules to which they conformed were arbitrarily imposed on them by their elders, so that when the day should come for release from control they could fling the yoke off their necks and live according to their desires. There was no mistaking the closeness of the relation between the home ethics and the august divine law. It is difficult to explain how this has come about—but both parents would certainly say that it has been granted in answer to persevering, heartfelt, utterly genuine prayer.

There is my reminiscence. It dates from a good many years, and though I have looked round me ever since, no quite parallel case has come into observation. Where there has been an approximation but yet a falling short, the difference seems to be due to the presence in the more ordinary family circle of our old friend the "swelled head." Some little trait of braggartry, of condescension, or worse still of indifference to the large issues of life, has indicated the presence of a root of bitterness which works a steady, unsuspected havoc in the higher life, just as in the relations between England and Ireland. But when I look back on the oasis lying fair among the drifts of barren sand, I am inclined to say: "Let no man dream that the establishment of a home such as this is out of his reach, for it is not."

Yours sincerely,

J.

Letter LI

Dear Henry,

A jotting on your second and third questions.

No. 2 relates to the old problem: is a business life compatible with a life of service of God? Undoubtedly, if "business" is a necessary of modern life. In that case many men will be called to it, and if they are called to it they ought to devote their whole powers to doing it as well as possible. But "well" doesn't necessarily mean what we call "successfully." The Christian business man is honest, diligent, cautious, enterprising and far-seeing, but he is never wholly absorbed in getting. Indeed he is far more interested in spending his money properly than in acquiring it plentifully. Very likely he is less opulent than he might have been, but if he is in any sense of the word a true follower of Christ, and (the same thing) knows why he is in this world, the question never occurs to him. He may be a man of few words, but all who know him know that he is a witness to the eternal truth of Christ's teaching about money, self-sacrifice, and the presence of God's kingdom everywhere in the world. There are not many such, but there might be; and the few there are do yeoman service in keeping mankind out of the pit.

No. 3. Self-expression. Your difficulty will disappear if you do not omit, what I omitted, corporate training. The boys of my model home learnt to feel the greatness of the fact of membership in the Church of Christ before they left home. Hence they unconsciously developed their own personalities by forgetting them in the service of the community, and at nineteen were not dependent on puerile reminiscences of house-football matches for their guidance into the citizenship of heaven. That is because the claim of the unseen has been continuously presented to them, and so the recognition of membership in a divine society is not a formula, nor a bit of cant, nor the token of a prig, nor the prating of a precocious bore, but the power in the young man which makes for self-forgetfulness and strong peace of mind.

All this hangs together and is wonderfully simple. Nor have I any doubt at all that each new generation is as receptive of truth as any that have been before. Why? Because the Almighty is amazingly patient with our waywardness and crass self-will; and shows it to us Englishmen by such gifts as skill in handicraft and native love of music, which persist on and on in spite of our stubborn and repeated efforts to kill them. So is the appetite in all of our normal children for God and for goodness. The soil is as good as ever, but where are the sowers of the seed?

Yours ever,

JAMES.

Letter LII

My dear J.,

I think I will adopt your suggestion of a provisional agreement. The fact is, the view presented is unfamiliar, and I am in the stage of requiring either some experience which would constrain me to a cordial assent, or time to ponder and co-ordinate before judging.

So proceed. It is clear that if Christianity is to be presented as a religion of joy there is danger of making it void of its stern side, which is not only very prominent in the Gospel but has affinities with the Puritan who slumbers within us English ready to be awaked again some day. Is it not evident also that the spasmodic attempts to make popular Christianity joyous, Pleasant Sunday Afternoons, short, "bright" sermons and services, and the laborious establishment of fellow feeling between the village parson and his flock through the medium of dances and social gatherings, are, if not disappointing, at least not the reason of the survival among us of the Religion of the Cross. These things may oil the wheels but they don't give motive power. Yet it is undeniable that what the Apostles brought to the people was a message full of hope and *stimulus*: it goaded the callous worldling but it did so not by scolding him so much as by setting before him a glorious thing within his reach. There is a grievous discrepancy here. Keep it in mind, will you, for treatment in due season?

Ever yours,
H.

Letter LIII

Dear H.,

You are perfectly right. One great problem of to-day is exactly what you have said: how to reconcile the awful sternness of Christianity with its radiant hope and joy; and I am glad you see the need of grappling with this problem before we feel prepared to set about training a child. For in thousands of cases, and in homes of piety and goodwill, godliness is presented in so confused a fashion that as soon as a youngster begins to think for himself he can see no light for his footsteps, and treats it as a venerable curiosity, an accessory to his ethical efforts which has something to be said for it; meantime a few very delightful people hold to it, but no clear-headed man looks upon it as indispensable for bringing joy into the lives of others. I have known some men and rather more women of whom this has been true; one in particular was a man who was never without a headache and frequently suffered aches and pains in his limbs. Yet he never entered a room without bringing something better than sunlight into it, and each time we came into touch with him we went away a little less inclined to think that life was in vain. We felt this without knowing of the grim background, but when we learnt what he endured, our vague exhilaration in his presence was lifted into something more like reverence and worship. For that power in a man to transmute suffering into the quickening of others is not of earth nor of man's conceiving; its purpose and its effect are more than human. It allows us to infer that the sufferings of the innocent, even when they seem to be restricted to the sufferer, are in some untraceable way redemptive for mankind.

It is not very difficult to see that for such a spiritual giant as St Paul this inference was a potent conviction; yet it never worked in him towards a self-complacent braggartry. It revealed the wondrous growth of his personality, but was quite free of what we call egoism.

Now does not this fact make it a little easier to understand how "all the noble army of martyrs" in varying degree ignore pain because of a sense of something which makes it a blessing, though at first it was conceived of as a curse? In short, it makes it possible to insist that if this view is derided as absurd, or Quixotic, or mystic, or unintelligible, the derision is due to an unconsciously mechanical theory of the Universe which, axiomatically, puts out of court all considerations not to be verified by the senses. We tend to decline downwards nowadays into a state of dull protest or hustling antagonism against anything that seems to bring us any contradicting of our ordinary natural inclinations. When in that humour this line of thought rouses in us a kind of mute indignation too deep to wish to justify itself at the bar of reason or common sense or piety or goodwill. But I am beginning to wander into philosophy, and I take it you are indisposed for any such journeying. Tell me then if you can stomach this nourishment so far.

Yours ever,

J.

Letter LIV

Dear J.,

I know you will make allowance for a brain no better than a fungus (as an old controversialist put it), if I hark back to the altruistic creed again. I find myself and others vacillating. We believe in altruism, but latterly I must admit I have had qualms not only about its practicability, and the power of its appeal, but the soundness of its foundations. I have been staggered by many instances of incredible hardheartedness shown by people of station and education, and by quite as many who have neither, in presence of the heartrending suffering caused by the war. Great Heavens! think of this. A wealthy couple were induced with much difficulty to lend their mansion as a hospital for officers. They were put to a slight inconvenience in moving to another quite as big and as comfortable. Round the first was a grand garden with many acres of kitchen produce. The lady gave the strictest orders that not one vegetable, flower or fruit was to be given to the hospital. Did you ever hear the like? But what is more to the point is, what is wrong with a society which can first breed and then tolerate such a woman? What has been her training? She must have heard the preaching about altruism again and again, and yet seems quite complacently to have turned a deaf ear. Now, mind you, there are thousands of the same ilk at large in this England of ours. It is ridiculous to shrug the shoulders and say the parents were at fault. Of course they were. But I have a suspicion that the creed is at fault, and, further, that it is because it somehow lacks the push of the religious impulse. For supposing one of the stony-hearted *canaille* looks you in the face and says: "You prefer to be unselfish, do you? Well, I don't, so there's an end of it." I confess I am cornered; and James, dear friend, how do I know that my boys are not going to turn out men of this type? If they do, what remains for me? Μὴ δῆτα πρὸς θεῶν, as Demosthenes used to say. Never have I felt more in need of your luminous counsel.

Yours ever,

H.

Letter LV

Henry, your appeal touches me to the quick. We have known each other for forty years, and for a good spell out of them I have seen the answer to your difficulty. How is it then that I have not passed it on to you? I have been wanting in the first duty of a friend, but thank Heaven, the opportunity is come now.

Hark back to my letter of about two months ago, where I gave an account of a self-indulgent youth's dilemma, about everybody, even the philanthropists, being self-pleasers. Your difficulty is the same as his, with the very noteworthy difference that he was rather happy at observing the fact; you are aghast at hearing of its outcome.

Now take careful notice of this. I don't impugn the quest of happiness because we have hitherto failed of success. It is illegitimate to assume that a desire is not right merely because it is difficult of attainment, or apparently impossible. The reason I taboo that quest as the purpose of our creation is that it always expresses a selfish aim, even when the word is construed by people in a very lofty and attractive sense. Moreover we can see the corruption of the self-aim as soon as we detect the fact. For consider: by happiness we mean the *feeling* of happiness. As soon then as that feeling languishes owing to the temporary failure of our quest, we are justified in our melancholy; undeniably so, since the failure of our *summum bonum* means that for us Creation is a mistake, a miscalculation—in fact a fraud. But to save ourselves from so harsh a word we postulate a general rectification in the next world and practically abandon hope for this. Hence disillusionment; irresistible because so rational.

Now excuse me if I explain further. Among the hordes of rather depressed men and women there moves one here and there who, though sorely buffeted in life and naturally sensitive, spreads joy wherever he goes. We admire him because we know he has overcome the very difficulties which we fancy are too many for ourselves. So the more we excuse ourselves the more we exalt them. Hence in vast numbers we feebly postpone our hope of rectification of life's ills till the next world, dreaming that our burden meantime grows because so few of us find happiness, the real reason being that so many seek it.

If personal happiness is ever rightly to be the first aim of a human being, then how absurd to distinguish between the aiming at happiness for others and our own selves! Why should there be any distinction? You cannot say it is because self-happiness is found to be a delusion; that is that the more A aims at making A happy the more certain he is to fail, but that as soon as he tries to make B happy he succeeds. No. He does not succeed. Look at the world. *Circumspice.* Why then do so many preach to A to set about making B happy? The answer is quite simple. They think that the mere endeavour whether it succeeds or not, will make A happy and possibly themselves as well! He is told to be altruistic for egoistic reasons, and in default of anything better he acts upon the exhortation strenuously for some years, and then of course more languidly as he finds that neither for B nor for himself, A, are things any better than they were.

Now shoot your shafts at this statement: the sharper the better. I invite them cordially.

Yours sincerely,
JAMES.

Letter LVI

My dear James,

I can go with you when you imply that happiness cheaply interpreted is merely a selfish way of living. But that is because it is a vulgar self-indulgence: £ s. d., soft ease and a hard heart, tenderness to self, coldness towards others. But the real thing called happiness. Why, I have heard in a sermon a striking description of the early Christians as a group in the midst of swarming votaries of pleasure, distinguished from them not for their irreproachableness of conduct so much as by their joyfulness. This was new to me, but I went back and hunted about the N.T. amazed at finding how ebullient and ever fresh must have been the deep draughts of happiness by which those men were sustained. Now are you going to tell me that we bewildered mortals are not to long for that unspeakably precious thing? And if we long for it are we not to pursue it? And if the right life is the pursuing of it then, clearly, we are right in training a child to pursue it; that is, we shall show him how true the old maxim is that honesty is the best policy, and that being kind to others is the way to find life worth living. Yet I am bound to say it was rather startling, only three days ago, to come upon a saying of Mazzini's, in a little book lying on the table in my dentist's waiting room. He is an unusual person, my dentist. He regales his expectant visitor not with unnameable picture papers three months old, but with a compact little volume of pithy sayings, and on my word I dived into it and almost forgot my special molar problem. Soon I came across the startling words of the prophet-patriot: "With the theory of Happiness, as the primary aim of existence, we shall only produce Egotists."

But am I to pin my faith on Mazzini for every *obiter dictum?* A go-ahead lady not many years ago, when confronted with some sentences of St Paul's, gaily replied: "Well, Paul isn't everybody." To judge from reviews, some leading divines are disposed to agree. But if you back up Mazzini I shall betake myself anew to the pastime of scratching my head and hoping for some new light to come of that time honoured way of bettering ourselves, derived, I suppose, from our Simian forbears.

Yours ever,
H.

Letter LVII

Dear H.,

To begin with: Happiness is not the same thing as the pursuit of it. Nor is the pursuit of it the same thing, necessarily, as the longing for it. Nor, again, is the longing for it the same thing as the devotion to it as if it were the only thing to be longed for.

But first we must be clear that we are talking about the same thing. Put aside all vulgar notions of happiness, aye, and away with even the most refined and civilized conceptions of it too, such as a "good" man might picture to himself as his grand hope in life: a career of useful and congenial work, success in high endeavour, a full, bright, harmonious, family circle and an honoured old age; and all along, and concomitant with this aim a good deal of self-denial, no great amount of luxury but of course comfort; and again all along, the ministrations of religion conformable to the temperament of himself and his children and servants. I say that this prospect must never be before any human being as the *first* aim in life, if he is to fulfil the purpose of his being brought into the world.

There are not many audiences who would not receive that statement with a howl of derision. But I am going to make a more extravagant one still. It is, that if a citizen as he reaches manhood, discerning the poison in that programme, namely its inherent selfishness tempered only by some not very whole-hearted altruistic activities, were to abandon the pursuit of happiness for himself and devote his whole energies to making other people happy *in that way*, he might be a real saint and a hero combined, but he would be giving himself to a vocation which would be pursued on a fundamentally false principle: the principle that a man's life does consist in the abundance of the things which he possesses. The exact opposite was affirmed and practised absolutely without qualification, stint or reserve by the only supreme Artist in the art of living that we have ever known.

Why then a saint and a hero? Simply because such a man engaged in such an endeavour may be acting on the highest principle that he knows, and with such singleness of heart that as he grows older all self-regard is destroyed in him. In character he is nearly perfect; but none the less his principle is false though it is the best he has ever heard of. For it assumes that man's happiness is the supreme thing; and that is false, no matter how refined and lofty the meaning of the word may be, or how sincerely it may be construed as blessing other people, not the self.

Now, most long-suffering of men, when you read this I suspect you may be just able to withhold yourself from the uttermost scorn and vituperation. You will point out that quite 99 per cent. of the foremost peoples of the earth cherish this ideal which I presumptuously denounce, as the noblest imaginable, and that no one without an inherited strain of lunacy in him would dare to slight it. But you will temper your language for one reason only. As a practical scheme it has failed. Perhaps for the prosaic reason that it requires a vast supply of the good things of this world, and that as a fact there is not enough of them to go round unless our desires are vastly modified. If you have any qualms about this or even if you have not, will you read attentively the second part of Browning's *Easter Day*? and after a dose of that let me know where you are.

Yours ever,

J.

Letter LVIII

Excuse a post card—I've read that Browning. Stupendous! But it seems to postulate a certain view of the end of the world which is very questionable and, I should have thought, out of date, and I still don't feel able to go as far as you seem inclined to. But let me be till I write again.

Letter LIX

Dear J.,

After scratching my own head for an hour or two a happy thought occurred to me—to scratch someone else's! I don't know if you have come across Lord Downham who wrote a book on *Ethics of Corporate Effort* some few years ago which, if I am not mistaken, was highly praised by some philosophical journal. So I sent him your letter giving brief information about the context and what has led up to it.

He was, of course, short of leisure, but I knew he would have something pointed to remark, so I transcribe his laconic comments: "Your friend is a tough customer. Assent to his question about all forms of selfishness being condemnable. He is right there—but pummel him further. Does he maintain that single-minded desire and effort for the happiness of others is wrong? His words on that question still 'gape for interpreters,' as Pindar said."

Pindar must have written in curious style if that phrase is typical, but I agree with your critic as to the "gaping" alluded to. You will have a job to convert the John Bull of the twentieth century to your point of view. That is anyhow certain.

Yours

H.

Letter LX

Dear H.,

Dogmatically but not reckoning without my host I will say my interpretation binds principle and practice more firmly together than any other possibly could.

Consider. There might be something to be said for the ideal of working for others' happiness if it weren't for the perversity of human nature. But (1) suppose happiness is taken by the others to mean material prosperity, your efforts to secure it—the more unselfish they are—must teach that material prosperity is the *summum bonum*; and that is just what it is not.

(2) Next, rather deeper. You may tell Harry and Phyllis, Dorothy and Tom to slave for others' happiness, but at the bottom of their young hearts is the objection that they prefer their own, and why shouldn't they? Then you will hastily don the costume of the sympathetic maiden aunt, or of the cheery broad-shouldered housemaster at the boys' public school and persuade them that the unselfish life is the road to happiness; that by altruism the ego is satisfied, which, as most boys will interpret it, is a miserable lie.

Of these two (1) is more practical than (2). But at the bottom of both there is the same disastrous fact. By mere altruism you teach something which is not true, and we are in this world to teach what is true and never anything else. What does experience say?

What does experience say? Did you ever read a well-written but dismal book called *Changes in the Village,* by Bourne, and do you recall the picture of the well-to-do villa people gradually settling themselves among the indigenous squatters, and taking trouble to make them happy? They provided entertainments, they distributed good things, etc., and the result was an increased estrangement and an ever deepening bitterness. Why? Not because the kindness was poisoned by condescension though it often was, but because the deadly mammonish view of life was taught in the most effective way. Mrs Openhand and her spick-and-span daughter get up a concert and let the squatters in cheap, having gone round the cabins previously to give invitations. How does the thing come into Hodge's mind? Why, of course, in this guise. He fancies them saying: "We, Mrs and Miss Openhand, having prudently and successfully looked after No. 1, are now in possession of the happiness we have sought, and we tell you that the best thing you, Hodge, can do is to seek it in the same way, abstaining from certain things but choosing others prudently as we have, and you will have your reward, as we have ours. We have not been slack, but keen and energetic in eliminating suffering from our lives, and now we want to help you to the same freedom for yours. Thank God, we don't want to keep our good things to ourselves." So says Mrs and so Miss; but what of Hodge? Why does he come to the concert and laugh at the paid and rather vulgar comic man, but go away soured and still hungering in his unnourished soul? Because he has a dim consciousness that for all the conscientious parade of altruism, the ideal of life which has been urged upon him is selfish. The divine spark within him has been nearly extinguished by his own Hodge-like service of Mammon; still he recognizes the pitiable counterfeit which has already beguiled him to his shame. Under the jam deftly spread by the Openhands he discerns the old swine-husk of self-pleasing, which he has already learnt to loathe. So good night.

Yours ever,

J.

Letter LXI

Dear James,

I have read your last with real attention twice, nay, thrice, because I am old enough—I mean young enough—to know that when a doctrine put forward strikes one as going too far it is very likely to shed light on the road one has already chosen. Am I right, now, in thinking you are knocking down the Happiness ideal, however it is interpreted? I mean that it is obviously true of all coarse conceptions of happiness. The people of whom it was said: Their god was their belly, were admittedly failures of education. But am I to lump in the same category with them those noble minded philanthropists whose labours have undeniably made life happier for millions of their fellow creatures? I write with diffidence when I touch on religion, but surely our parson was right last Sunday in saying that the foul conditions of life which obtained 100 years ago and still are deplorably common, cannot be in accordance with God's will. Well, doesn't that mean that they are to be remedied? If so, the man who remedies them has attained the ideal of making people happier than they were before; others therefore are right in aiming at the same ideal. *Q.E.D.* All seems to me to depend on our having a fairly high idea of happiness and to be ready for self-sacrifice in securing it. That oversets your argument and is a tough nut to crack.

Yours ever,
H.

Letter LXII

Henry, my patient friend, I heard the other day of an Oxford disputant of whom it was said that when he was either worsted in argument or was tired with too much football, his replies took the form of repeating the last thing he had said, only louder. Now I am not accusing you of so disputing—though I could conceive that some acrid critics if they wanted to pick— well, well, I leave that; let us put it this way, that your last letter makes it hard for *me* not to repeat what I have said, and said at some length. But I will be on my guard.

Will you face fairly the question whether all forms of selfishness are not equally to be condemned? Perhaps you would say, not equally. Well then let us say simply, condemned. Now I am not charging philanthropists with being selfish men in disguise, though of course some of them may be. That is not my indictment against the happiness-ideal of life. I detest and dread that ideal for two reasons, one practical, the other theoretical, and these are they:

(1) You justly observe that the ideal in question can be fairly judged only if the word happiness is made to connote something high. Very good. But suppose people won't or anyhow don't interpret it so? My misgiving is based on plain observation of fact. For, in obedience to the social demand that we should set ourselves to the task of making others happier, we find each man, or group of men, construes the word in his own

sense, viz.: as satisfaction of his particular desires with regard to life in this world, of whatever sort or level they may be. (I say "in this world" because an imperious demand has been made on serious-minded people not to fix their gaze so exclusively as heretofore on the next world, but to deal vigorously and sanatively with this.) And who is to prevent him?

(2) The reason why the outcome of all the happiness-philanthropy is deplorable is that it is virtually an appeal to the self-regarding instincts of those who are thought to be badly off; a stimulus of those instincts, and finally, their disappointment. It is all very well distinguishing between happiness and pleasure, and labelling the former as good and the other as bad; the facts might justify the distinction but nearly always do not. Unless something like a miracle has happened John Doe construes the former word just as Richard Roe does, i.e. as something wanted by the self for the self and capable of being secured if prudently pursued; whereas by a law not to be traversed or ignored, it can only be secured on condition that it is not pursued, but forgotten or merged in the quest for the real thing.

Can you discern this? Note that a quest, a desire, an ideal, is good not according as it takes a useful direction or starts a desirable reform of outward conditions, but in so far as it is inspired by something higher than, and different from, the self. But many Johns and Richards and their wives, desire a general easing of others' distress, often, not always, because it would mean an easing of their own. Their hearts are bruised by the sights and sounds of mankind's unmistakable woe; let alone that the state of things is nowadays not only pitiable but menacing. Nor is this diagnosis disproved by the existence of a chosen few who forget themselves in the striving for others' happiness. Their idea of happiness may be the common conventional one of less suffering; but, if their self can be forgotten in the effort for others' welfare, then you see a rare and beautiful thing, the unreflecting, un-selfregarding man. But mark it well—if he is truly unselfish it must be because he has hold of that something which is higher than self and different from it, though he may not know it. What that is we shall see, I hope.

Meantime, one word more. You have to estimate not only the motive of the philanthropist but the effect of his action on those whom he is trying to benefit. Now it is hardly possible that the aim of the active philanthropist should be construed by those whom he tries to help as something higher than what is in their own minds. Their notion of happiness is egoistic, and so they interpret his motive as egoistic. Or if his unselfishness is so lofty and strong as to be unmistakable, that makes no difference in their view of the kind of happiness he is trying to establish. They cannot help thinking well of a man according as he sacrifices himself in order that they may gratify themselves. In other words, self-forgetful kindness on his part and steadfast endeavour to make life easy for them are in their judgment the ideal of virtue? Ask Hopkins, your neighbouring parson, if such estimates are not plentiful among his people. The cynical of them think he gets a better salary if he fills his church; the others know only one word of praise for him, that is, "kind"; while "standoffish" or the like denotes the utmost blame.

How far do you agree with this?

Yours ever,

J.

Letter LXIII

Well, J., dear friend, I have gone far enough to feel the salutary annoyance and unrest which are always for an Englishman the accompaniments of a new idea stealing into his mind. Creighton used to say the discomfort of this experience made the recipient at once try to get rid of the pest by writing either to his bishop or to *The Times*; and that he himself used to suppose he would best aid the applicant in his wish for a return to quiet life, if he threw the letter, to which the intrusive new idea had been committed, into the waste paper basket. Do you propose I should follow this example? Please go on.

Yours,

H.

Letter LXIV

Dear Henry,

The analogy of bodily health will guide us. We agree that the pursuit of our ideal should be single-minded, unvacillating, constant, and that nevertheless if that ideal is bodily health, the human being loses his with a certainty in proportion to his concentration. "Yes, but how if he forgets his own body and devotes himself entirely to the welfare of his neighbours' bodies? Isn't that all right?" I demur.

When we advise each other about health we are playing with fire. The best chance of safety is to suggest remedies indirectly, else the neurosis is confirmed and the sanity of mind and body alike is fearfully jeopardized.

Now if there lurks such a deadly poison in the study and cultivation of so beautiful a thing as health, why not in that of happiness? Don't accuse me of preaching that we should be slack in trying to help our neighbours. Far from it. But I do preach that there is no true succour given by any adviser of his fellowmen to those in distress unless he turns their thoughts from the ego to something higher. If any advice or influence which contradicts this law seems to succeed temporarily—as of course it may—

'Tis as the ivy leaves around the ruined turret wreathe;
All green and wildly fresh without, but worn and gray beneath.

But isn't it time we tackled the question of this "higher thing"? What is it? What guarantee is there for supposing that there is in it a power mighty enough and delicate enough to cope with this subtle arch-dissembler the human ego? The peril of this warfare lies in the intimacy of the attack: the ego is emphatically within us, as we might say. In earlier days the popular idea of the devil tended to obscure the fact that if the kingdom of God is within you, so is the kingdom of Satan. We used to think of the latter as safely outside of us, whereas I suppose it is both, like the other kingdom.

Yours ever,

J.

Letter LXV

Dear J.,

I sent your last to Theophilus who *more suo* replies on a postcard in Greek, Latin and French. A nephew of mine staying here fresh from his scholar's laurels at Trinity helped me over one stile, and I gather the translation is as follows:

"Your *homunculus* (don't be offended!) means by the 'higher

thing' man's relation to God. Extract from him how this meets
the difficulty of egoism; warn him against magic. We don't
haunt the Ilissus, but the Thames by London Bridge; and his
remedy must be *nescio quid Tamesini*. The health analogy is
sound."

The nephew says the cryptic Latin phrase means "must
smack of the Thames," i.e. be English, modern and practical;
not remote or fanciful or dreamlike or antique. I hope this is
plain. For myself I can just in a struggling fashion hold on to
your analogy; and what it really suggests is that the pursuit of
happiness—however the word be interpreted—is a selfish business unless it is transformed by being made indirect; that is, by
being made the corollary of the higher quest. Is that right?

Yours,

H.

Letter LXVI

Yes, Henry, you are right and so is your friend, in spite
of his gibe at my stature. Let us then take up his challenge.

The more attentively the aberrations, blunderings, criminali-
ties, lunacies of mankind are studied the more it may be discerned that egoism is at the bottom of them all. In some shape
or form every misguided man sets himself to pamper or exalt
the ego. But you can pamper the ego in two ways. The simpleton
gratifies, as far as he can, the appetites, the five senses; the more
complex man prefers something more refined in the way of
sensation. He either contemplates his own faculties while in
exercise, or gets other people to do so, deriving a subtle pleasure
from the thought of their admiration, and fancying he can live
on that honey till he is summoned elsewhither.

Such conduct is more contemptible than comic. But why is it
either? Because it is a clumsy, humbugging way of displaying
the self. True; but that is no explanation. It is an unaccountable
fact that self-display is not only a mistake because it fails of its
object; it is far more. It is a practice which at first is bearable if
it is cunningly dissembled, but it becomes, as soon as dissimula-
tion is suspected, either comic or nauseating or both. Such is the
bore, as we call him, the terrifying person one meets with in

hotels who will talk about himself with all gravity and copious-
ness of detail till patient spinsters flee before him as from a main
sewer.

But why shouldn't he talk about himself? One often com-
plains of someone talking of things he knows nothing about; but
of himself surely a man knows anyhow more than other people
do. It is his special subject, and even a bore is tolerable sometimes
if you get him on to a subject he really knows, but only on condition it is not himself.

Now meet a man in Kensington High Street and put this
question to him and he shows impatience. To him it requires no
answer; not because he dislikes the effort of finding an answer,
though he does, but because he thinks the answer obvious and
requires no effort, or even mention. But that is because it rests on
an universal law which can only be explained by a pure assumption, though it operates in general experience. That it invariably
operates seems to justify us in not trying to explain it. Whether
that is so or not, its invariability deepens its mystery.

Observe, I am expatiating for a moment on what your friend
calls the "difficulty of egoism." He meant the difficulty of combating it; but before we come to that we must realize the difficulty of explaining it. "We fight not against flesh or blood," etc.
Nichts geheuer ist es hier. While then, talking about oneself is
silly and offensive, habitually acting for the self is abominable,
and persistently thinking about it is nothing less than incipient
insanity, and even short of that, is inexplicably weakening. But
there is a power always exhibited by real unself-consciousness.
Think of an actor, a child, a public speaker, a candid friend, in
short, almost anyone in any surroundings who wants to do something difficult.

These and a myriad other facts converge upon a law which
may be thus stated: the self, if it is not to be a bane, must be
ignored; not till it is ignored does it show its true power.

But when we try to act upon that law, life's pilgrimage remains an exceedingly difficult matter. It is as if a man were
walking along a narrow track through a quagmire in the dark,
and various friends, knowing the singular fact that a somnam-
bulist plants his footsteps unerringly, owing apparently to his
unconsciousness of self, tells the pedestrian to do likewise. "For

your own sake forget yourself." But he answers testily: "What are you at with your crazy counselling? You bid me forget myself for the sake of myself. What is the sense of that? At one moment you shout to me to be wide awake, the next you tell me to walk like a man in his sleep. I daresay it would be desirable to be two persons at once. But who is to do it? and has it ever been done? Yet the benefit to myself is so palpable, so undeniably worth striving after, that I will not give over the attempt, and in the pursuit of *my* happiness and in the hope of *my* progress I will try to forget *my*self." Then his friends call to him over the marshy flats which surround the path and bid him not worry about his own happiness or his own power of seeing like a cat in the dark, but to give himself to helping others. As the path is so narrow he could best do this by telling them to follow him, but as his own progress is grievously slow he prefers to exhort them, using the same odd appeal as that to which he is accustomed, "pursue your own happiness by forgetting yourself; walk like a man in his sleep, but be wide awake, always." The effect of that is they all flounder alike. Most fortunately for these pedestrians every false step jolts and jerks them out of equanimity and makes them think there is something wrong. If it weren't for this they would have been engulfed in the mire long ago.

Now, Henry, the difficulty of the real pilgrimage of life is far more subtle than the clumsy figure, into which my garrulity has betrayed me, would suggest.

It is that the reward of well-doing is so wonderfully congenial, suited and attractive to the doer that it is almost more than human nature can achieve, not to grasp at the reward and by trying to appropriate it, lose it. To put it as simply as possible, notice the 119th Psalm. It is an expression of bliss, of spiritual exhilaration, of the uplifting of man's whole being which comes of fixing the thoughts on that side of divine revelation which we think of as law. Observe for instance verse 106, one of many. "I have sworn and am stedfastly purposed to keep (ponder on) Thy righteous judgments." Why? because of my conviction that that is the highest life, not the life of mere busy effort but of contemplation of the part of God's revelation of Himself, which appeals to us under the guise of an unvarying and exacting demand. But if we set our thoughts on them *because* thereby we gain happiness we fail to gain it: that is part of the law. Yet the very gloriousness of the reward almost compels us to put it before ourselves as the *summum bonum*. We are constrained, not by the simple fact that we are caught up into the divine, but by what we know are, or will be, our sensations when it happens. The moment we set our desires on the felicity which we cannot help anticipating, we forget that which is to be our "All in All," and so lose it. It is the Life in the Eternal, that is, in God Himself, Who is a "jealous" God and will not allow man to put anything in his thoughts before Himself. I don't believe that you or any other honest-hearted man really doubts this. Very well, then, apply it to the canon that the highest form of human endeavour is the greatest happiness of the greatest number, leaving self out, and how does the canon look? Let me hear.

Yours ever,
J.

Letter LXVII

Dear J.,

I write at once lest you should forget a sentence in your last which for my limping intelligence demands amplification. It is about the "gloriousness of the reward." If a reward divinely offered is, as of course it must be, glorious, can there be anything wrong in desiring it? If we desire it may we not strive for it with all intentness? Happiness is the reward of right living. If right living is the giving of happiness to others, obviously it is free from selfishness, and how could we do better in bringing up a child than by setting his affections and desires on this unselfish happiness? Excuse this abruptness. Somebody is just ringing me up.

Yours,
H.

Letter LXVIII

My dear Henry,

Your question would be hard to answer if the choice were between things on the same level. But what we are discussing is a choice between giving ourselves to the Eternal God Himself, the Infinite Giver of Life, and on the other hand to that which is after all a feeling only, the happiness which the self-surrender invariably brings. It is so inevitable a concomitant of the surrender that we may look on it as a help; but the moment it is put first it becomes not only a hindrance but an impassable barrier. It might be a help to an astronomer eager to learn about the sun, to study the light cast by the sun's reflexion. But if he wishes to know the sun itself he had better give over the study of the reflexion, else he will go on to scrutinize the shadows and end by loving darkness rather than light. What then?

But I would rather forgo any explanation of an analytical character. I maintain that we may discern, or anyhow live by, a law without being able to analyze or explain it; and that we have to live this universe whether we understand it or not, or rather we shall never understand it unless we first live it.

Observe, in passing, that there is a type of temperament which refrains from wrestling with the law, but peacefully contemplates others in their wrestling or non-wrestling. It is of the passive and receptive sort, takes the world "as it comes," and if it is of the observant kind and is endowed with a rich power of expression you get a potential Shakespeare. That bard eludes all scrutiny because he hides his selection. We may almost say that he scanned all types of character with such sympathy that you cannot tell which he preferred. He points out which come to a bad end in the world as it is, but his astounding justness of observation seems to be a compensation for the lack of the highest thing, burning love, which means a consuming eagerness to select the best and ignore the second best. But "back to the muttons."

If we are right in distinguishing the pursuit of happiness for the self from the self-surrender to God as opposites incompatible with each other—God and Mammon—and further, that every child begins by interpreting life wholly in respect of his inclinations, you see the meaning of education; and why Christ laid stress on one practical social precept, viz. "Go ye and teach." That is to say, unless some constraining ideal higher than self but truly congenial to it is held before the child by his elders he inevitably sets to work to serve himself with eagerness or languor according as he is active or passive by nature. Now comes the question again. Granting that, and that Mammon is Hell, may we not be content with an ideal which is not religious but unselfish, namely the pursuit of happiness for others?

I say No, and I trust that what I have written will partly justify the negative. Add the following.

We are considering a social question; not only the effect of a certain ideal on *A*, but on *B*, *C*, *D*, if *A* follows it and induces others to follow it. Now, we agree that if *A* pursues his own happiness as an ideal, he makes a mess of life. What then if he is altruistic and doesn't think of himself? One very serious consequence is involved. He teaches others the very ideal which he shuns as poisonous for himself. Happiness, as I have said, is a word we all construe differently. For nearly everybody it includes *as an essential condition* material goods together with health, friends, etc., in fair abundance. Now I ask you: Is it possible for *A* who has those goods and relishes them as we all must, to busy himself about securing them for *B*, *C*, *D*, who have them not, without teaching *B*, *C*, *D*, most effectively that the goods are the things of most value in life; especially as they have probably a strong predisposition to believe that creed, never having been effectively taught anything better? Further than that there is nothing better except—what?

Yours ever,

J.

Letter LXIX

Dear J.,

Once again, feeling somewhat inadequate, I tramped off to "the shining parterre and trim pleasure ground," where I reckoned on finding our good bishop. He is one of the very few really hard-working men who manages to think. How he does it nobody knows; but every time I see him I find him penetrating deeper than before into matters not only of moment, but of present-day urgency. His interests are those of all of us, and in despite of incessant racketing, rushings hither and thither in the diocesan motor, lumps of recurrent legal obligations which he may not delegate and cannot adequately fulfil; a hard sawdusty pile of jobs which would have choked the rising flame in young W. S.'s capacious soul, yet one may come upon him able to bring his deep tranquil mind freshly on any bugbear which poor harassed worldlings, be they anaemic widows or flustered shareholders, it makes no difference, may bring to him in hope of peace. Seldom do they fail to hear of it, though his balm curiously enough has a bitter taste for all its consolation, and while his counsel helps you to act wisely it sends you home again feeling a bit of a fool. Funny thing this; however, here is what he said. I write it down from memory in the privacy of the boskage in his shrubbery:

"Your friend has 'touched the thing with his needle point,' but has not quite finished his answer to your question. You asked him: 'Why should we not be contentedly altruistic, switch our energies off from selfish to unselfish happiness and without more ado spend our lives for our friends?' He points out rightly that while we abjure self we should still be preaching it. Practically, he says that is inevitable, but I think if you worry him a little further, in his patience he will give you something deeper and more satisfying; less critical, more constructive. Try." So here I am, trying again.

Yours ever,

H.

Letter LXX

My dear Henry,

There is no escape from the abortiveness, the recurrent failure, which dogs the footsteps of the votary of happiness, except by self-committal to something higher and more constraining, yet free from the poison which infects the self-ideal, invested with the living power which belongs only to the personal. It must be capable of the most intimate appropriation, but if grasped, as by right of ownership, it crumbles away. It is the life eternal offered to us as an inexhaustibly glorious and transforming blessing on condition that our allegiance to it is pure and free from all selfish aim. What can that be but God Himself?

Now mark this: light is thrown on the paradox of our relation to the Divine, our reception of that which is plainly not ourselves, yet so intimate as to become ourselves, by the rather weird pronouncements of psychotherapy. Truth comes to us from without, but is modified apparently in our subconscious mind before it becomes part of our conscious mental furniture. We are taught to-day that all "suggestion" which seems to come altogether from outside and to be so potent for cure, only operates from within the self and that too on condition of the self being forgotten. There is something almost terrifying in the manifoldness of God's appeal to us all to recognize always far more than we ever do the activity of His beneficence. The appeal now is to those who cannot think of anything but their own health. They are sickly in mind as well as in body, and here is a new way of learning His great prescription: that we should drink in what is offered us from without, and which yet is inward from the very start. All suggestion is auto-suggestion—a startling parable of the means of grace!

You see the point? Do observe how this principle lights up the educational problem. From the very beginning onwards it challenges the parent to get his boy to interpret life in terms of devotion to a Person; any other rule of living is Nehushtan. When once you take in the hopelessness of any other endeavour; the terrific fact that it has not only been a failure in combating evil, but is itself a fruitful cause of evil, being the most captivating quickener of all misdirected zeal; you will recognize that there is no tragedy to compare with it. Character of lustrous beauty, talents of royal splendour, hopes unquenchable and constancy not to be daunted; all have been devoted to an enterprise which was never for a moment contemplated or countenanced by our great Exemplar, and such as it would be a profanation to imagine was ever in the thought of the Apostle of the Gentiles. This sort of undertaking is habitually extolled as "practical Christianity." Its effect, and very often its purpose, is to sanction exactly that interpretation of life which Christ suffered in agony to extirpate from our minds for ever. I would take off my hat any day to many of the workers in this perversely-conceived crusade, for they are doing the best they know; but woe be to the society which has allowed them to grow up believing that to make the world lovable for all these random drifting hordes of humanity is the same thing as to transform it through the power of the Holy Spirit liberated to action by faith in the Crucified Saviour.

But there now! You wanted something more constructive and I have only given you criticism. But I will let it stand. Therefore, when I say that for a child the only power that can save him from his self-regarding instincts is his Maker, don't be irritated as if I were prating folly, but think if the phrase be true.

My good friend Horace White has had a house now for some years at Rockborough College, and tells me that when he receives a youngster from a really good home—alack! how rare!— he is dumbfounded at the beautiful blend of the inner boy with something from outside, an interpenetration of personality unlike any other known to man. There is something in the child so intimately his own that it is part of himself, not a constraint from above; not a fettering, nor a goad, but an inward invigoration not to be described, an interfusion of the divine with the human, which is a nullity and an illusion if it be thought of as human, or if it be held as a simply divine, wholly detached abstraction.

There is something most appallingly presumptuous as well as profane in man's self-congratulation. Yet our instinctive revolt from it how unreasonable! unless it be true—literally vitally true—that the improvement we can't help noticing in ourselves—though we ought to help it—is God's work. No doubt, in word we acknowledge this to be so, but

> Who for that one brief moment hath descried Him
> Dimly and faintly hidden and afar

can help being sickened and terrified at the ease with which in our peacock-strutting we display our Creator's bounty in the hope of capturing some of man's lunatic applause? Grotesque such "beholding of vanity" must always be, but it is ghastly when it concerns the utterly sacred mystery of a soul's cleansing, or the training of child.

If then It is a reality and can be apprehended by a child as It certainly can, it must be as a Person. The inanimate has no voice that a child can hear.

Can you go with me to this point? I hope so. Write, dear friend, dipping your steel nib deep in candour.

Yours always,

JAMES.

Letter LXXI

My dear James,

I begin to see that up till now I have been conceiving of education as if it meant simply the leaving of the child to grow naturally, only supplying nourishment. But I cannot gainsay the force of your statement of what the danger is. It is palpably evident that as self-love is the grand antagonist to self-giving there is a terrible peril wrapped up in these two facts, true of every child: (1) that nature prompts him most constrainingly to love himself; (2) that if this self-love is prudently guided it conforms itself to worldly opinion and becomes acceptable, amiable, attractive, so that the world adds its own weight of false opinion to the force of Nature; and to oppose this combination we parents bring nothing except some fragmentary teaching about Christ, from which the element of self-sacrifice, the Cross to wit, is more and more excluded. If this is a true diagnosis of the situation it is nothing short of a miracle that Christianity survives. But it certainly does, and may be seen afresh in its own perspective.

So, do go on to the practical question again: the beginnings of religious training, and let me state a difficulty. There are many fathers of young children to whom your counsels would seem too lofty, too religious in tone to be acceptable. Yet they are good men, thank heaven. I can now see what you mean, but will they?

Yours ever,
HENRY.

Letter LXXII

My dear Henry,

Doubtless it is as you say. For a good while it is possible to jog along in question of conduct shoulder to shoulder with all sorts and conditions of one's fellowmen: quasi-Agnostics, impulsive spinsters, hard-bitten traders from the north, whimsical old ladies who consecrate the time they can spare from their lap-dogs to collecting fables about the ten tribes and the Millennium; in short all types of philanthropic tag-rag. But the time comes when it is necessary to bring God into the matter, and is it odd that it should make a difference? Education is one thing if you imagine that man does it, quite another if you realize that all that is vital, and that has in it permanence and promise is the work of the Eternal, Almighty Creator, through and in man.

Nor is this an irrelevant platitude. The unfailing characteristic of the divine action is that it is perfectly human. That is of course a blessed fact, but notice the danger that looms. It is not only possible but incredibly easy to fall into a mawkish piety, attributing in word, the result to God in an abstract fashion, not discerning the part played by man. Read what St Paul said about himself and Apostles planting and watering, but God giving the increase. If my gardener were to prate about the Creator making the roses grow I should suspect he had been sleeping too long in the morning and that either the planting or watering had been omitted. It is easy to play the sluggard, and then blame the Most High when no blossoms appear. What then is the part in training a child which man must play if the child is to grow?

That is no high-faluting question but plain business. Yet the answer will be wholly different according as we recognize or do not recognize both the divine and the human action. We have to act with scrupulous care and thoroughness but never meticulously as if our feeble blunderings were real helps to the Almighty. Philip and Andrew could not have supposed that Christ *required* the loaves and fishes, yet they offered them, and had they done otherwise the 5000 would have fainted on the way home.

If God is a fact, He is immeasurably the greatest fact of all. Education is the dislodging of the love of self by the recognizing of God. It is a very gradual process in which father and son co-operate with unfailing success as long as they perceive that by themselves they can do nothing. The moment we forget our own helplessness, our thoughts become profanity, our words drivel, and our actions idiotic. Moreover in this island, wherein you and I are living for a spell, it is far more likely that we exaggerate the human element than that we over-estimate the divine. Now, to apply these saws to the problem before us.

But, *sat lusibus indulsi.*

Yours ever,

JAMES.

Letter LXXIII

Ah! my dear friend, you have shown me what we all, *nous autres pères*, ought to have done! How many of us have done it? In our portentous blindness we have fancied that if the mere parental authority is enough for the sheltered life of early boyhood it will therefore suffice for the fending off of the world's spell in later life, when the youth leaves his home and his school and fares forth on his solitary pilgrimage. Great Heavens! What fools we are! How often I have heard good, wise, grave and kindly folk lay down without one note of hesitation the proposition that adolescence is the most impressionable time of life! Stuff, surely, unmitigated stuff. The fact clearly is that the entrance on manhood is normally, the time when the training of the first ten years begins to be revealed. The character—no! let us say the inner disposition—was then set either to self or to service; the feet were planted then on the downhill or the uphill road, and after proceeding a few furlongs the pilgrim shows on which he is walking and intends to walk. How terrific, by the way, are the symptoms of persistency in the will to be wrong!

Now a further big question looms at this point. I want to be clearer on the connexion between moral and religious training, which nowadays I find are sundered, in theory at least and in most conventional quarters. Is there not some way of bringing conduct to illustrate the teaching about God?

Yours ever,

H.

Letter LXXIV

My dear friend,

You can't get good conduct from a boy in order to build religion on it. If there is a God, our relation to Him is the paramount matter, and it must come first in rank and in time. All good conduct is based on that relation.

But the words must be understood. Look at the facts. A child born selfish finds that pleasure accompanies self-gratification, and for some few years he shapes his life accordingly. This shaping is interrupted by vetoes from the mother to which he finds it best to conform, and if they are consistent enough to be intelligible he speedily forms "good" habits, i.e. those which don't make his elders' life intolerable. This is called discipline, but it is a surface affair in that it leaves the fundamental creed of life undisturbed. Supposing then that after a year or two some ordinary religious notions about God are given him, the question has to be put: do they raise or absorb or transform this self-regarding creed or not? All depends on the view of God which is imparted. Popular Christianity teaches that if the child behaves well things will go well with him later; and so he tries to be "good," i.e. what his parents require, and hopes for the best. But by twenty-five years of age he discovers that the "best" does not come as he had hoped, and so he gives up *inter alia* going to church where he is expected to praise God—the Giver who does not give. Being honest-hearted probably, and spiritually indolent certainly, he is delighted to find society does not disapprove of his shirking church; the only pleasure, as a cynic said, which never palls. (That is because the instinctive sense of its being a bit wrong persists for years; if the grown man could really persuade himself that it was right the pleasure would vanish.)

So much for the popular "Christian" training. You will note that the creed of self-pleasing includes God, who is expected to minister to the creature's needs in return for respectability of conduct—a ghastly travesty of the real thing. But what is the real thing? Simply a new Life offered: the truth being planted that the law which the parents enforce comes from the Unseen Personal Father. Very little talking is needed; but an initial statement, coupled with the sight of the two parents kneeling in prayer to show that they are submissive to the same Law, is the sure and adequate starting point. As time goes on, any symptoms of lawlessness demand a tiny reference in the evening prayer, and that must be seen to. The grand peril is that the parents' authority may be and often is deemed to be sufficient; that is, no steady guidance is given to make the youngster see, feel and know that the moral law comes from God through the parents. Till this comes about the religious teaching is nearly bound to be all gas.

I'm sadly pressed for time to-day, so I've been brief and dogmatic. Is it fairly clear?

Yours,

J.

Letter LXXV

Dear J.,

If I understand you, it comes to this. The human babe is born selfish, and it requires a strongly constraining power to get him to subordinate this instinct to a higher. That power at first resides in the parents. After a time, but quite early, the law that they enforce ought to be referred to a heavenly source. This of course assumes the existence of God and is probably an effective way of teaching it. Is that the reason why you recommend that method? Because it seems to me it may after all be superfluous. The parents' authority is often quite sufficient for the formation of good habits, even on to eighteen or twenty, through all the slippery time of life. If that is so, and when it is, then surely morals being in a way selfsupporting will grow to be divorced from religion, which is the very thing we wish to avoid; but need it be so?

Yours,

HENRY.

Letter LXXVI

Why, Henry, you are reverting to an exploded superstition. You are putting the virtue of the boy first and God is brought in as a buttress to it. That is *au fond* either Atheism or Idolatry or both. Keep hold of the primeval teaching: "I the Lord thy God am a *jealous* God," that is, all true conception of God recognizes that His claims on man are paramount simply for His sake, and not for any blessing that obedience to them will bring. The standing tragedy of human life may be summed up in the words "He comes unto His own, and His own receive Him not." The tragedy, I say, not because life is shorn of all its lustre but for the fact in itself. "In knowledge of Whom standeth our eternal life." Do let us try to discard all considerations of the ruin that attends on ignoring God, immeasurable and inevitable though it be. In that fact there is death but in the knowledge of Him eternal life. If God is God how could it be otherwise? and what more do you want?

But all the same you are gripping the essential truth that what we want to give the child is not a theory but a life—a relation to a Person, not to a hypothesis. Dear me! One reads some of the wonderfully able, acute, balancing, treatises, setting forth the reason why on the whole we should incline to believe that a Mind has been at work in making this universe. The writers seem to pride themselves on being unemotional, and some of them apparently find consolation for life's rubs by decrying emotion in other people. Emotion wrongly directed is doubtless a tiresome thing, sometimes silly, sometimes amusing, but never, I think, very harmful. There are times, anyhow, when worse than any emotion is the absence of it, and one of those is when man's soul turns to the Author of its being; its stay in trouble and its hope of salvation. If at such a time the soul can remain unmoved it is either because it is yearning after a phantom, or is accomplishing the feat of turning truth itself to sawdust.

Now let me write you the last great saw with which I set out to trouble you. The education of a child, intellectual, moral and even physical, is summed up in one process. It is the setting of him off on the quest for the Eternal, the Life-giver, the Redeemer from all sin, the Stay of all true virtue, the Fountain of all truth, the Author of all beauty. By birth he enters on his heritage of delusion, the belief I mean that love of self is to be his only guide and hope. What we have to do for him is so to kindle his affections for the higher life that his seeking for his Father shall never fail or his desire grow cold. As he seeks he will be changed, "transformed by the renewing of his mind," as one said who knew what he was talking about. Your intellectual onlooker will tell you that all training is the imparting in due season of a set of correct propositions. Each selects those he prefers; the most illuminated of these pundits, while declaiming against sacred propositions, which they call dogma, pin their faith on scientific propositions which they call knowledge; only insisting that these shall be imparted gradually as the growing mind can receive them. But meantime the human boy requires and insists on securing for himself allegiance to a person. If you don't show him a personal God, he will choose another person to worship, and the one generally available is his Self. That is what I call Mammon. As long as he remains a votary of that cult he is imbibing the poison which corrupts his desires and degrades every aspiration, and so distorts all his vision that he no longer sees anything as it is, and all secular knowledge must become to him a pack of lies.

But my language is becoming unparliamentary. The wind must have shifted to the east, for my chimney is smoking. But what I have said is none the less true.

Yours always,

JAMES.

Letter LXXVII

My dear James,

It is all very well your saying that you have given me your "last saw," but it opens out two questions, one for the second time. (1) As long as man remains at all selfish, all secular knowledge comes to him "as a pack of lies." That is a bit sweeping; one of those dicta which seem to follow logically from what has been admitted, and yet can hardly express a living, actual fact. Anyhow it would lead us into a huge morass of enquiry, and I vote that we postpone it for a convenient season, for the subject is the effect of the divine Life upon intellectual conceptions. (2) You bring me once more on to our old friend, the principle that self-sacrifice must be unlimited or it is nothing. That is I think involved in your last. "A quest for the Eternal" obviously makes any drawing of lines inadmissible. For while all advance means ignoring of self, the limiting of moral endeavour at any point whatsoever is a violent act of self-assertion.

But note this. How on earth is that compatible with social life? We can't give up everything, and when once you settle to keep some things—a fairly comfortable house; a decent tall hat; books, etc.; enough money to travel, etc.—you postulate liberty of action which your canon and the Sermon on the Mount alike forbid. *Que faire?* Holy men seem sincere except in this, and we wanderers are puzzled, and the "Labour" world scoffs.

In haste,

H.

Letter LXXVIII

A p.c., Henry, in answer to yours.

I am not laying down what Tom, Dick and Harry are to do, but what not to do. Self-surrender certainly involves a lot of renunciation; but how much, and what form of it are questions left to the individual. The contradiction in this of the Sermon on the Mount is only apparent.

Put this into your pipe. I will send you a line to-morrow.

J.

Letter LXXIX

Now, long-suffering Henry, I must hasten on; and you will allow me to be curt and dogmatic.

"All knowledge is a verification of assumptions," says H. Spencer in a burst of inspiration. Every child, not idiotic, assumes the uniformity of nature, though much evidence contradicts it; and in proportion as he assumes it, he acts upon it; then by acting on it, he learns some of its qualifications, but presses on ever on the same assumption, finding there the secret of learning.

Coincidently with this he assumes his parents' love, and for a short while it suffices to uplift him; indeed if it be combined with the enforcement of law and helped by the schoolmaster it may serve as "the master light of his seeing" till he begins to interpret life for himself. Then at eighteen or so he faces life afresh. The influence of school and home wanes, and the drama of his life depends on whether he has taken on a higher creed than self-interest or not. If not, he may become a fairly useful citizen and even an attractive man, but, as they say of Kaffir boys, he soon ceases to grow in mind, and never reaches the stature which has all along been within his vision but outside of his desire.

All Nature and all experience convince us that the only safeguard against this woeful shortcoming is to lay a foundation of living conviction in a child's mind of the existence of a Personal, Unseen, Heavenly Father, Who deals with us all by Law and Love; and this knowledge comes normally and easily through the parents who for the time being are *in loco Dei,* but who fail egregiously in their vocation if they adopt the fashionable line of making all morals depend on *their* guidance and approval instead of basing that approval as early and as firmly as may be on God's Law. Convention urges them to go no further, but unless they do they are almost sure to leave Nature's creed fundamentally undisturbed. For the youngster's notion of God is merely that of an indulgent caterer, on whom he can reckon for "a good time" if he conforms to the canons of worldly respectability.

Now notice: the growth of the boy in so far as it has been genuine has been through self-forgetfulness; by using the evidence of his senses, yet always correcting them; the fatal error has been in letting him think that this self-forgetfulness may harmlessly cease at a sort of agreed-upon point, beyond which if anyone goes, there will be many who will think him a little mad, or anyhow a crank, or "wanting in sympathy," because "the world" means the many millions who labour to persuade themselves and others that life is meant to be lived on this method of drawing the line. But the hard fact is that the moment we draw that line, we cease to live and begin to perish.

Yours ever,

J.

Letter LXXX

Thanks many, James; let me now make a shot at some practical desiderata, based on your big principle that growth in life means forgetfulness of self, or what the Bible would, I suppose, call "dying" to self, or to sin. Every time a sensible father enforces a prohibition in his household, he is interrupting and so undermining the child's inclination towards self-pleasing. This is the essential ingredient in all good training. But even more salutary as moral training is the encouragement of wholesome activity, which by its objective purport can keep selfconsciousness at bay, and secure the ascetic element not through silly self-inflicted pains, but through joyous and unreflective and at the right age corporate self-expression. If moral training is to be wholesome if must be of that truly healthy type. Now Christianity as presented to us when we were boys was mainly prohibitive, and those of us who were alive kicked at it, while those who conformed were generally the well-disposed but anaemic group. Have you any "tips" as to the quickening of unconscious activity, not only in childhood when it is very easy but through early adolescence when blushing begins, along with gawkiness and other troubles? I am told by my schoolmaster friends that the tumult of the period called puberty is more marked among boys than girls, baffling enough though it often is among them too. If so, our housemasters in the big boarding-schools have silently taken on themselves an Atlantean burden.

Ever yours,
H.

Letter LXXXI

Dear H.,

Just as no mortal knows whether in the history of language the word precedes the idea or the idea the word, so we cannot tell whether good action is coincident with right thinking or succeeds it as a consequence. Consider. Our baby takes to sucking his thumb at eight months old. His mother takes steps to stop it, by interposing gently but firmly on each occasion. The child after some resistance and with energetic protest obeys. A small matter, but it contains the whole essence of many ethical treatises. The beginning seems to be the loving action of the higher life on the lower; the tone of admonition—though not one word is, so to speak, understood—is at first caressing, but if unavailing glides to reproof; and if needful may go so far as to shape itself into something that might almost be called a slap, a rudimentary cuff or tap or stroke. So much for the action from above. Now let us think of Master Johnnie again. He ends this little conflict by abstaining from the tabooed thing, and the diminutive thumb remains unsucked for all time. But while Johnnie abstains chiefly from a wish to be on good terms with his mother, Tommy will think only of the cuff, not minding particularly who it is that administered it. Each deals trenchantly and decisively with ethical principles, not weighing them but acting on them; and the whole drama of a soul's story is in our microcosm. If Johnnie were a perfect child his appetites would be rampant and strong, but stronger still the desire to win the mother's smile. Tommy, on the other hand, is in for a long combat with the flesh; the spiritual motive is at present weaker than the physical, and he construes the mother's action (his experience) not as an appeal to his affection, but as a threat of bodily discomfort. He gives the primary place among motives to the bodily sensation which experience has taught him to expect. There it all is: God *or* Mammon. One *or* the other is first, not both, nor neither.

N.B.—The conflict is between flesh and spirit; flesh meaning what I take it St Paul meant: the desires of the lower life which of course may be spiritual; pride being the broad term to describe them. If either Tommy or Johnny is vigorous and has the makings of something great in him, the desire to assert the self will be very strong, but stronger still the yearning for the mother's love. The child from whom little or nothing is to be hoped is the one in whom both sets of desires are languid. That is the beginning of the lukewarm man.

Now let us perpend the parent, and we shall find that she too has her conflict. Mrs *A* notices the thumb-sucking, and, being a practical busy woman, jumps to the remedy which promises most to her and administers the rap forthwith, omitting the caressing. That was the pre-Victorian parent, rare to-day. That is the beginning of a legal training, the law without the Gospel. We all know its defects, and in trying to avoid it we fall into the other extreme, love without law. For Mrs *B* disbelieves in punishment, nagging and the like, and has learnt to prate about interest, persuasiveness, loving kindness, etc., not knowing, poor soul, that love without severity is not worthy of the great name of Love. It is mere sentimentality; a shoddy, slobbering thing, though attractive to the twentieth century mind. So her Tommy, finding nothing unpleasant comes of disobedience, sucks on, till the desire dies, giving place to another more mischievous. From that time he condemns thumb-sucking as childish, but he is growing to be confirmed in sensuality.

Johnnie meantime after enough rappings changes his habits but not his view of life. He still seeks gratification but avoids sundry piggish little tricks as costing too much, though there is nothing yet that displaces his innate selfishness; and even his change of behaviour may be only temporary, as long as he is *in statu pupillari*. Anyhow he is steadily set on acquisition of some kind. No boy is without inclinations, though I have heard of some who want nothing except to be left alone. Whatever they are, if he grows up more determined to gratify them than he is determined on anything else, he is on his way to the abyss, and a vast multitude keep him company.

The problem plainly is how to turn his desires away from self. There is a false but very plausible way of tackling this little matter. You notice how Nature chimes with common-sense and the Gospel. At about twelve years old a boy takes naturally to corporate play, and thus in boarding-schools, not necessarily in day schools, gregariousness comes to the rescue just in time to stem the rising tide of egoism which sets in with puberty. Schoolmasters have often defended athletics for the wrong reason; as if hard exercise counteracted sensuality. This is very doubtful. It is the corporate spirit that wars effectively against ego-worship, the foster-nurse of sensuality and all devilry among young and old. Sensible parents too encourage corporate play earlier in life for the same reason, though generally not knowing why. (You may note how in education as in building the British Empire we do our best things without a notion what we are about.) But in many of our arrangements for the young, especially in the holidays, we let ego-worship work untrammelled. The very interest taken in childhood and in growing but undecipherable boys plays Old Harry with the character by turning the thoughts inwards. If the principle of self-abnegation were better understood we should quickly alter many things in education, for it is easier to make facilities for others' self-forgetfulness than to forget ourselves.

But how absurdly we fail to notice that in all this we only aim at provision for childhood and adolescence, whereas the period of most dismal and visible deterioration is that of early manhood when the youth quits both school and home at once and faces Mammon in all its glory, seductive and compelling, glozing and threatening, penetrating and massive, all at once! Yet it is idle to cast about for expedients to suit young twenty year olds who have been deprived of the *elixir vitae* so far. They are doomed to be flotsam on the stream of life unless sharp calamity and disillusionment befall them opportunely. For the seductions of the world are manifold and very potent. They appeal to what is noble and generous and of high aspiration in the newcomer. "Do that, be that, and we will honour you," and all the time the ideal is a phantom.

Or the tempter touches his indolent disposition. "Be a spectator; record what you see and you will make a name as a writer; we like to read what is well written, no matter whether it is true or not; and of course you will avoid the common error of preaching?" Compassed about with this and 10,000 other shadows, how is the callow juvenile to keep on the Narrow Way? He cannot, will not, does not, unless he is aware by experience of a Presence before which his false self shrivels while his true self expands. How is that experience given?

It is perfectly simple though difficult. Everything that happens to him is capable of being interpreted so as to make God more and more of a reality and less and less of a mere imagination. But the interpretation must be rudimentary or, rather, elementary enough to touch his experience and knowledge. If it is above them and out of range, it will come to his mind as something false, however truly it be expressed. It is a tremendous fact, and a warning that truths are effectively imparted by one to another, not, as we ridiculously imagine, by words alone, but when the recipient's mind works actively, assimilating the testimony of all the senses, not only of the ear. In other words, experience is indispensable, else the words fall short.

Thus the first intimation of the existence of God should come to a child not as Richter advises, through a thunderclap, but by visible proof that his parents are submissive to an unseen Father. Note in passing that the knowledge gives him nothing new, but only strengthens immensely what he knew before: that his parents have been to him already the inspiration of all true thought as well as of all true action, and it is because of this native trustfulness in them—a pure divine gift—that Jesus said "of such is the Kingdom of Heaven." Moreover the trust should be in both parents. People have said pretty things about prayers learnt at the mother's knee. But what of the father's all the time? Why should his knee be omitted from the picture? It is certain that if the mother alone be the channel of the divine knowledge there is a grave risk of Love being taught to the exclusion of Law: kindliness without severity, affection without discipline. To avoid this the mother is saddled with a very heavy burden. She has to play a part for which Nature has not equipped her, though Grace may, and here and there visibly does, do so. But mother of the Gracchi are not found in every street nor in every green valley.

On this theme pardon a further descant. All knowledge of the Unseen World—the higher life—comes to us in a sort of double guise; to one child rather terrible, to another rather lovable. Yet the same tidings. If either element is partially suppressed the injury to the child may be immeasurably great, and I am afraid often proves irreparable. But one is far more likely to be fatal than the other. I mean that if a mother chooses to be lax in discipline she will do far more harm than if she is over severe, for she will be corroborating the soft view of life already planted by nature, which if it is to be corrected must be corrected by real discipline, real severity. You will spare the rod at the peril of the boy's soul; spare the lollipops and no harm is done. Notice, I beg you, that what is at stake is the foundation view of *all* life. We can hardly conceive the beautiful freedom from prejudice with which a child starts on living. He is really prepared to believe that life is not all beer and skittles, though he hopes of course that it may prove to be. Leave him alone and he will try to make it such.

Hence the marvel, which yet is no marvel, that a huge proportion of our greatest men have been the sons of country parsons—I maintain that few more valuable truths have ever come to light; but it clamours for interpretation first, application next. What was distinctive in those homes? Many things, as compared with ours now, but at all times they have been marked by certain characteristics: (1) the child has seen a lot of his father; (2) both parents have been visibly engaged in working for the unseen life, till its claims on the children begin to assert themselves vigorously; (3) life is unexciting, no racket of amusement, but self-resourcefulness, encouraged by children being left alone; (4) obedience insisted on; (5) country-life, and unconscious communing with Nature. These five characteristics are not trifles. They are very big things indeed, for they help to manifest the Eternal. We have thrown them nearly all away, the idea being apparently that the Eternal makes no difference. *Vive Valeque.*

JAMES.

Letter LXXXII

Carissime! That fact about the country parson is illuminating. What fools we have been, to be sure! Most of all in this, that we hate to be shown our faults; that is, we try to make out that it is God's fault, not ours. I see no consolation in that.

Meantime a practical point. You advocate and rightly the simple life. But how is it possible? Not only are children born luxury-seekers, but if I want to be sensible, what of my neighbours? Am I to forbid Jack every lawn tennis party because they will give him claret cup? and plunge him into discontent, when he sees young Harman riding a new bike, which I have just refused to buy? This is by far the most serious practical difficulty of any. The county families are *capables de tout*, and the *nouveaux riches* even more so. What then?

Yours,

H.

Letter LXXXIII

My dear H.,

I verily believe I have come to the bourn. You might have started ten or a dozen objections to my nostrums, but there would be one answer to them all which I will do my best to state.

For each of us in life a work is provided, which we cannot fail to make a heinous mess of if and in proportion as we conceive wrongly about God. To give us the opportunity of a right conception is the special work of the Church on the human side. We are concerned just now with the conception of the Divine taskmaster, and we have to learn that the higher the task that is prescribed the more uncertain, at the start, is the issue, by which I mean the more dubious appears to common sense the prospect of success. It is exactly herein that its true vitality lies, for work undertaken resolutely and with buoyant hope when all sagacious critics can discern nothing ahead but failure anyhow is not born of self-regard. Its greatness and its fruitfulness consist in its being God-inspired, for it starts free of all false hopes, which suggest the kind of success of which there is no mention in God's portfolio of instructions. Those mighty heroes in the art of living, Isaiah, Jeremiah and Ezekiel, started on a work of teaching though they knew at first that they would be scorned for certain, and probably persecuted and possibly killed.

So in your problem beware of over-rating practical difficulties. *They really are not arguments against, but for, the course proposed.* For think how clear must the call be which sounds through all the Siren voices, and wins its way to our reluctant ears! Neighbours! Of course they will raise their eyebrows and shrug their shoulders and turn up their noses at you, and perhaps do all three things at once! But if in spite of this ungenial prospect you find yourself impelled to try the simple life for your bairns, well, try it in Heaven's name unflinchingly. See that no servant ever does anything for them which they can possibly do for themselves, and let this be the normal state of things, thoroughly understood before any child takes in that it is exceptional. Read Booker Washington's autobiography and see what the surmounting of obstacles does for grit of character. Catch, moreover, something of the primitive sternness shown by Frederick Temple's mother, and long before your youngsters learn to expect this life to be all jam and treacle, they will have got accustomed to "do without." All this is training for a life which is to be a warfare against self or it will be a woeful tragedy: "One more sorrow for Angels," etc. Mankind seems incapable of learning how inevitably *all* softness of surroundings—not all beauty—rivets the soul of the child to earth. How can you expect him ever to be convinced of the hollowness and fallacy of worldly joys if you let him think not only that life is to be all enjoyment, but also that his elders are set upon making it so?

Mind, Henry, the jeers of the unthinking multitude are pretty good indications that the line I propose to you is right. Certain it is they will jeer, and I trust that you will "suck thereout no small advantage." I mean that it will be a sign-post showing you that you are right. Freeman, I believe, said of Froude that his readers could not fail to learn some history from his pages, viz.: that there was one way things did not happen, and that was the way Froude said they did. So I say about methods of education. It is terribly difficult to know which method is right, but the approval of the unthinking world at least shows you which method is wrong. And how could it be otherwise? The world's view of life is worldly; that is, we want this earth to be a comfortable place to live in. We have plunged into an abysmal quagmire by making comfort our chief aim, and then have been mad enough to believe that the end can be attained by leaving our children to grow up egoists. It is conceivable, though very improbable, that the Gehenna now yawning just ahead of us may convince a few of us that Christ was right after all!

Goodbye! old friend. I wish you God-speed in the noblest work that can engage the mind of man: the guiding of the growth of your own children.

Yours affectionately,
J.

Letter LXXXIV

My dear James,

Before answering your last I must tell you of an instructive experience. You know my boy Jack is at one of our highly spoken-of, highly fee'd preparatory schools, and after thinking over our discussions or, rather, some of your recent letters, I thought I would pay the place a visit and see what is happening about religious teaching. The headmaster is an attractive specimen of a muscular Christian and good man of business; everything about him and round his school and in it smacks of healthiness and sane virility—a marvellously better establishment than the one I was at in Brighton in the eighties. But the place of religion in the teaching puzzled me. Instead of its being, as I remember it, supposed to permeate all the lessons and all the life of the place, I find it has 50 minutes allotted to it on Monday morning, 40 minutes on Sunday afternoon, and the rest of the week is secular.

Now I admit that our Brighton theory was theory only. What the permeation amounted to was a pure fraud. The whole week was secular; but I fancy the idea was traditional and that our ancestors were brought up under it for weal or woe. How does it happen that these and similar changes in education have come to pass in this country without anybody knowing what is going on, or any of the agents in the matter knowing why the thing is happening at all? Do tell me what you think. The separation between sacred and secular, whatever be the quality of the teaching on Sunday or Monday, must, I should say, give the boys a pretty definite impression that God has nothing to do with science, history, etc., but that His dealing actively with the affairs of the world came to an end many years ago, at the Reformation perhaps, or, more probably as they will have heard of it, at the Battle of Waterloo. I don't feel easy about it.

Yours ever,

H.

Letter LXXXV

I cannot feel surprised at your misgivings, Henry; the change you speak of marks what I should call a gradual and mainly silent revolution in English minds. Since the Middle Ages a vast increase in our knowledge of the world, of Nature, history and art has taken place. Whether rightly or wrongly we have abandoned the idea that all the teaching a child required is the rudiments of Christianity and enough Latin to enable him to understand the Church Services; and in place of that notion we thrust a mass of information down the boys' throats, aye and latterly down the girls' throats too, though no one concerned has the slightest confidence that more than a fraction of it is digested; but everybody knows pretty well that what is not digested is bound to be injurious. The chaos which results is indescribable and gets worse year by year as the influence of outside examinations on the schools becomes more irresistible. Ask any headmaster who knows black from white and he will tell you that the intellectual training of all classes of young folk to-day is a miserable business, for the reason among several others that everything is done in a hurry, and fewer and fewer boys can profit by it. I could write reams on this melancholy subject, but it does not concern you directly as a parent except as regards the modern attitude towards religion in schools. You see this is how things stand. There would be a terrible indictment to be laid against headmasters and others who control the teaching if there were anybody who did control it. A swarm of pundits at the universities are nominally responsible for the mass of subjects required of the schools. In reality it is the result of a singular conviction in the minds of all men and most women who have reached a high position from their proficiency in any one subject, viz. that as their own moral and mental excellence is known to all men, it must be due to the subject they learnt at school and college. Further, that as it has been so successful in their case it must be imposed on all young people for all time; that no matter what social changes may come about, or how different one mind is from another, or how many other subjects go to the wall, or are retained in fragments just enough to swear by (and swear at!) their particular subject must go on for ever. That is anyhow ensured. Everybody groans; nobody knows who is responsible. The one thing certain is that since this multiplication of subjects began, young Englishmen are if possible more unintellectual than ever. Outside the classrooms some really valuable training goes on. Nobody knows much about this; when they do they will try to destroy it. But inside the classrooms!

Infandum regina jubes renovare dolorem! Shall I go on? I have not yet come to your question about the sacred and secular. Appalling though the mischief of congestion is, there is another far more poisonous and more radical, and it is almost undetected to this day. It is closely connected with your question.

Yours ever,

J.

Letter LXXXVI

Excuse p.c. I have no idea what your deeper mischief can be. The other I knew something about; bad enough in good sooth. What can be worse? Unveil your bogey.

H.

Letter LXXXVII

My dear H.,

This is my bogey. You see how the idea of a subject being "secular" has come into the general mind. But is there such a thing as a secular subject? Can there be any knowledge of anything worth knowing which does not shed some light on the attributes of God, if we are right in supposing that He is the source of all truth?

Some thinking person with a little time on his hands—do you know of one? I don't—ought to prosecute a searching enquiry into this matter. Till it is done—and I see no prospect of such an event—I shall maintain what you will call a paradox, viz. (*a*) that there is no subject which if learnt on the theistic assumption does not enrich and purify our ideas of God. *Per contra*, (*b*) there is no subject which, if taught wholly without reference to God, will not instil falsehoods into the learners' minds.

(*a*) This requires no corroboration, except that some might say mathematics, pure or applied, is manifestly unconnected with religion. Of course it is unconnected with worship and with questions of morals. But when rightly taught—that is, when each advance means not a new mastery over the technique, but a new idea of the relations of numbers, of the laws of space and of motion, etc., it must suggest thoughts about the Maker of the Universe which inspire wonder, and anything that does that is theistic.

But the proposition becomes more self-evident if we consider (*b*). Take science taught atheistically (N.B.—that adverb does not mean openly denying God, but keeping silence about Him; by far the most effective way of teaching that He does not matter. It is because so many millions of parents have kept silence to their children about God, that so many adults are saying, Tush, how shall God perceive it...? and are turning earth into hell.)

Science is the knowledge of order, of harmony, purpose, which we call development in the right direction, or evolution. But without God how can there be a right direction? Or anyhow, can anyone give any scientific *proof* that things are developing to a glorious goal? Certainly not. What right then have we to talk of evolution? None whatever unless we feel sure we are right in affirming as a big truth what we cannot prove. Now as we *all* constantly make that assumption, what is there to dispute about? Nothing, except one strange fact, viz. that many teachers of science are continually hammering into their pupils that no really sensible fellow ever assumes what he cannot prove. That is their fundamental principle of procedure. But notice how Gilbertian a business it all is! A science teacher begins his lectures, we will suppose, with a caution often to be repeated, against any assumptions that can't be proved. Having delivered himself of this bit of orthodoxy, he proceeds to harangue about the glorious development of the universe, including man, towards a distant but wholly satisfying goal; that is the doctrine called evolution. He might if he liked stick to the bare meaning of the word and assume the development to be in the opposite direction, downwards; not Heavenwards, but Hellwards. The only drawback to that policy would be that before long his class would walk out of the room. They couldn't stick it, and if they did it would be because they didn't understand a word he was saying; but then his reputation as a teacher would take long to establish; indeed he would probably be bowed off and betake himself to another sphere.

Now think. You and I agree that the teaching of truth is the teaching of order. But the teaching of a clever man who contradicts his own canon is a teaching of disorder; that is, of a lie; and if he does so without knowing what he is doing he does it all the more effectively. But he rouses a stiff resentment in that minority of his pupils who have learnt to believe from experience in God as a living person. For the teaching of the clever man they know ought to be self-evident, but all the time their sub-conscious minds—I mean of course those that are truly theistic —are telling them that much of his prating is stuff and nonsense. That is to say, they are being taught more nonsense in the science laboratory, if possible, than elsewhere; a disappointing result after having been promised the exact opposite.

There are two ways out of this hobble, one false, the other true. (1) The former is for the teacher to asseverate again and again, whenever, in short, he has nothing else to talk about, that his canon only refers to things within the horizon of science; that can be sensibly tested; but that there is a vast region of existence outside that horizon with which for the next hour they, as scientific people, have nothing to do. But some of the boys soon smell a rat; they suspect that this outside region has something to do with God, and cannot conceive why the teacher should warn them off it. Till they can answer that question they are being taught to believe the universe is a chaos, at least that part of it which comes into their school hours; just as their comrades on the classical side seriously believe that the *Aeneid* was put together by some hack round the corner, who was paid a fair sum as he succeeded in writing absolute nonsense from beginning to end.

(2) The other way is to assume that nearly all the class believe simply, but not very deeply, in a Creator, and to keep on linking the beautiful evidences of law, in chemistry, physics, or natural history, with their conviction that He is a God of Order, Beauty, Truth, etc. Any teacher who does this finds that English boys are finely equipped for science, and the reason why there is so little scientific interest in the country is that the teachers have struggled hard to put asunder what God has joined, viz. science and religion. Thus as English boys are I believe the most deeply religious of any in the world, or not far off it, they experience an unconscious antipathy towards a subject which, as far as they can tell, flouts or ignores their most intimate convictions. Of course I need hardly say they are as profoundly unconscious of what is going on as their teachers.

But I must stop. This is only one subject out of several. Mind, Henry, that you grip my meaning. If there is a Creator of this Universe, to teach young fellows its laws without alluding to His existence is mad and bad enough, but it is made much worse by many of the teachers assuming His governance of the world and pretending they are doing nothing of the kind. In proportion as they are efficient teachers, their rotten principles block the two chief avenues of truth to a young mind. That's not a small achievement for one life time!

Yours ever,

JAMES.

Letter LXXXVIII

My dear J.,

Most interesting what you tell me. How did you ever find it out? I have been pondering on it, but can't find any improbability in your diagnosis. However it affects the schools more than the homes, I suppose you would say; or rather would it be true to infer that more responsibility than ever is thrown upon the home? I fear so, but there was quite enough for my taste before. But have you gathered anything as serious about history teaching?

Yours ever,

H.

Letter LXXXIX

My dear Henry.

Some magazine articles on the controversy between scientific people and the orthodox, gave me the scent for following the matter up, and I met a very smart young science master lately at a public dinner, and elicited from him what really goes on. It is worth mentioning that in his opinion there is less reluctance to bring God into the matter than there was. So we must be thankful for small mercies.

As to history, you have only to read the school books or indeed any German, French or English histories to see what use we make of our own past. I can't conceive anything more interesting if the reader and the writer both see that our deep instinctive feeling for God makes us estimate one set of men's thoughts, aspirations and hopes as in themselves higher and nobler than others, and history tells us what sort of attempt our forbears made to realize those ideas as living things, not as spun out of man's imagination; to realize them being to rise nearer to God. That anyhow is the only way you can illuminate the records for a young mind. He blindly craves to connect anything that captivates him with his deep but vague notions about God. Great deeds of great men captivate him in his boyhood, especially if they tell of self-conquest, bridling of appetite, resolute striving after an ideal of generous self-giving, fortitude and tenderness combined. But think how the opportunity is lost! Why weren't we told that these lofty achievements were simply the manifestation of the Christ in man; the same divine, glorious thing that is promised to every baptized schoolboy; and that the response that he makes to the story is the answer of life within him to life outside or lived long ago, but present with us yearning mortals to-day, indestructible, purifying, uplifting and free; the Kingdom of Heaven within us, which our Father has given us the power to recognize and adore? No sooner do you keep all reference to God out of the lecture-room, and make, as most teachers certainly do, proficiency in history to consist in accurate reproduction of facts coloured so as to magnify human foresight or national greatness, and what do your lessons become?

They become a random narrative of interminable human blunderings, of the jostling, angry competitions of semi-animal swarms of living creatures terribly like ourselves in time past, repeated over and over again in spite of warnings distinctly heard and known to be irrefragably true, of racial recrimination, strife and agony in the horrible clutching after the phantoms of wealth and ease, combined all the time with an immovable conviction that the whole mad endeavour is a flouting of the very law of our true life, the very essence of the purpose of our creation. There is your choice. I know of course that many schoolmasters would say they keep the fact of an ideal of conduct before the boys without mentioning the name of the Deity, and that is all that is necessary. I reply that what Christ taught with the utmost emphasis was that we are in this world in order to learn to love God as a Person, not to refer to Him now and then as an ideal. Further, that the young mind can understand a person, but makes a very poor job of an ideal. Pardon vehemence. *Facit indignatio versum.*

Yours,

J.

Letter XC

But, my dear J., your vehemence is not out of place if your contentions are sound, and I don't see anything tangible to be urged against them. I sent your letter to the new Dean of ——, who has lately been studying the Italian philosopher, Croce, and he writes pithily: "Good sense, delivered *ore rotundo.* Perhaps the deepest plea is that history, to be worth anything, must be the story of the *thoughts* of mankind. Why are men's thoughts interesting? Because as he says, we have a solid conviction that some thoughts are higher than others, and the enquiry how far our forefathers, or indeed anyone, strove to reach the higher thoughts, or paltered with them, or pressed on through them to

others higher still, must always be a thrilling study. Why?
Because our power of valuing one set of thoughts, hopes, aspirations, etc., above another is a divinely implanted faculty; so
also is the human interest which leads us to exercise it and apply
the result to our estimates of mankind's doings 'here below.'"

Now this strikes me as germane to the issue. It gives an answer
along with yours to the question: "Why do we read history?"
But clearly the purpose of it is only discerned by those who keep
the ideal vividly before them. In fact, James, I am beginning to
believe that any study, contemplation, meditation, or briefly
any knowledge that is not knowledge of God is knowledge of a
lie or, if that is impossible, not knowledge at all. Somebody told
me recently that a big and learned divine, by name Hort, has
said that secular knowledge is only useful as showing us what
knowledge of God must be, and how it is acquired. I doubt if
many of our great academical people would agree. What think
you?

Yours ever,
H.

Letter XCI

Yes, my dear H., Hort was right, and very unwilling am
I to suppose he was ever wrong. He was a man of massive
learning, humility and piety, submitting his really powerful
intellect to be a handmaid of faith, in the search for truth, and
his book called *The Way, the Truth, the Life*, is a great master-
piece.

If I had time it might be worth while to show how the same
criterion should be applied to the study of other subjects, such
as literature, art and mathematics.

Deductively we are brought to believe that as God is all
Truth, the more we study literature in contact with Him the
more truth we extract from it. But there is this also: the beauty
in language is like the beauty in scenery or in art, not a thing to
be enjoyed independently of Him, but a gift from Him which
when understood may be enjoyed all the more as a manifestation
of His Presence; that is, it appeals to some minds with strange
power, while they are nearly deaf to the appeal of art or even of

Nature. But notice: just as a sunrise has a message for a child of God, who receives it thankfully, which message is missed by the arrogant, who receives it as his own discovery, so with literature, music, etc. A deeper, richer meaning of these things is discerned by the godly student, but a student can hardly be godly if the subject is taught as a "secular" subject, and I am afraid our boys are predisposed to look on it in the wrong light merely by the fact that the time-table classifies the subjects on a totally false principle. On the other hand, how surprising it is, though it need not be, that many a young fellow on being "converted" learns to detach himself more and more from the world, though at the same time and worked on by the same influence he detects far more beauty in the world than ever before! With mathematics I am less familiar and would speak with caution, but there must be some connexion between the fact that the universe is run on a mathematical basis and exemplifies laws which it costs us many a toilsome life of study to grasp; and the Mind of the Creator, which in other words must be through and through mathematical, and if His mind is mathematical so are ours. That is to say, the object of learning mathematics is not to acquire a mastery of some very intricate machinery or to hammer out proofs of self-evident propositions, but to be brought into the presence of great laws, which are manifested in and are the theme of the 119th Psalm, part of the material of a great religious poet's ecstasy. If this were understood, a mathematical lesson would be a very different thing from what you and I remember when we were left to flounder in the morass of algebraic factors and the forest of finite trickeries only devised as instruments for professional men, while we were hungering for the new and immense idea which was set forth not many pages ahead. Oh! the miserable waste of it! Yet we had minds!

Yours ever,

J.

P.S.—We may summarize this part of the subject quite briefly: All fresh perception of truth is a perception of the unity underlying diversity. That unity is God; the diversity therefore is only apparent. Hence to split up subjects into sacred and secular is to seek nourishment in a pestiferous delusion.

Letter XCII

Dear James,

I am doing a shameless thing in reopening our correspondence, when you have already given me more counsel than I can possibly carry. But a brief conversation with a public schoolmaster whom I met in a golf tournament three days ago has made me uneasy. In fact, I have been off my drive ever since. He has had a long experience as House Master at ——, and as, of course, I was pumping him about boys' training he dropped the significant caution: "Look into the food question." "What!" I said, "do you mean that the lads are still underfed?" "Not at all," said he, "they are over fed; but the public will have it so; and the few schoolmasters who know the truth are powerless." I was taken aback, never having supposed that growing boys can eat too much. Do you know anything of the subject? To save trouble, if you could refer me to an expert I should be most grateful.

Yours ever,

Henry.

Letter XCIII

My dear Henry,

Delighted to hear from you again. Do tell me how Jack is getting along; but whether the news is good, bad or indifferent, you must not expect me to climb down from the principles I gave you before. The more I think over them the truer I see them to be, though I admit I should now deal with questions more from the corporate than the individual standpoint. That is to say, we Christians ought to clear our minds as to whether we are or are not empowered by the Spirit of God to live a regenerate life, or only a natural life. For if we believe in the former something like a transformation may take place, and for that we are all yearning though we don't all know it.

But about this food. Once I consulted a really thoughtful physician, my difficulty being that a huge number of young men of all classes, and of middle-aged men, married, make a terrible mess of their lives by succumbing to the temptations to animalism, which they think of as really irresistible, especially *in re* the conjugal relation. It was evident to me that while a considerable number of young folk are free from the worst fleshly dangers, the number who are not is very large; and further, that there are very many who, though they do not actually succumb, yet are grievously hampered by the needlessly prolonged and defiling conflict. Lastly, I had misgivings about the prevailing ignorance especially among mothers (and few fathers nowadays count!) in that there is a general consensus that growing boys require "plenty of food." Putting these facts together, I thought it more than probable that an excessive and stimulating diet may be adding fuel to this most awful flame of sensuality: the vice which, Dr F. Temple said quite truly, causes more misery to mankind than any.

So I got my leech to write his opinion down, as it was sufficiently alarming and weighty. This was his letter:

"There is no sort of doubt to my mind that an excess of food, especially meat, which is heating to the blood, is a cause of the appalling severity of the temptation to fleshly sin among boys and young men. It is not a merely physical effect; the most deadly fact about it is the defilement of thought and desire and general view of life. If you could have heard what young men have told me! fine lads once, but now! The beginning of the melancholy tragedy is that early in boyhood the desires are inflamed, and the mothers, in ignorance, get the boys to believe that in the matter of food no self-control is demanded, whereas of course there is no department of life where such heart-rending havoc is caused if the law of the Cross is ignored. Infinitely wider and deeper than is known even to-day, this evil works. Why, then, you will ask, do not doctors crusade against it? Because for reasons I could give you there is a strong convention in the medical profession against our giving advice till we are asked, and then it is nearly always too late. My hands are tied, but if there is anything you can do, in Heaven's name do it!"

I have no doubt whatever that he is right. You will remember that I used to urge on you a change of mind as far more important than any reform of conduct. But when knowledge and reflection clearly point to a reform of practice, *especially if convention is against it*, no one who is not a sham can hesitate. The problem is perfectly simple. You have to face the fact that it is very likely your boy is rather greedy and that you won't be able to supervise all his feeding. Very well. It is plain that excess in a clean vegetable diet is less injurious than excess in meat. Therefore bring up your boys to be vegetarians, and if it helps matters that you should set the example, why not?

Yours ever,

JAMES.

Letter XCIV

My dear James,

I can go many lengths with you, but this vegetarian business is *un peu trop fort*. I don't gather that you back up your physician friend in his exhortation to *all* fathers to upset their households, worry about strange dishes and vex their cook into resigning, join the pallid army of puffy weaklings distended by brussels sprouts and potatoes, make themselves nuisances to every hostess, become praters about food, the most nauseating tribe of bores that walk the surface of this planet; and all because meat is supposed to stir the animal within us. Where is the evidence? He hardly hints at any, and against him there is the unquestioned fact that vegetable-feeding races are just as sensual as Europeans; probably more so, and that, I maintain, disposes of the whole of his argument. No, no! you have changed my opinions on a good many subjects, but there is something about this suggestion which scares me clean in the opposite direction. Why, your cabbage-feeder is a caution in himself; he is not only a flaccid variety of crank, but there is much of the real prig about him; he chortles about his own health, but what is it to me if he is healthy or not? and what right has he got to come gassing at me about my private habits? Give me the solid not the flabby food; the sturdy, ruddy-cheeked old-fashioned Saxon type of man of the sort who built up the Empire. On my word I can't away with it.

Yours ever,

H.

Letter XCV

My dear Henry,

It is a fact of rich significance that of all the topics dealt with in our long and varied correspondence, some of them sounding the very depths of our ethical, social and religious consciousness, the only proposition which has thrown you off your balance should be one that touches your diet. The proposition is that you should feel it to be reasonable for you to consider whether in the interests of your boys you ought not to become a vegetarian. Contrast the size, the scope, the eternal aspect of this subject with those of some others. You have quietly searched your heart to understand your own motives in regard to the maintaining of your true relation to your Creator. You have seen the miserable insufficiency of the modern moral code to afford a sound basis of a child's education. You have shown an alert readiness to take a wholly new point of view in matters of deep import and personal intimacy, and all with unruffled serenity of mind. But when it comes to a guarded hint that possibly a modification of your eating arrangements might be anyhow considered, whereby you would abandon the consumption of twice-dead animal flesh for that of the living clean produce of the earth, you foam at the mouth!

Not that I am in the least surprised. There is hardly an Englishman alive who enjoys fair health who would not do the same.

Your arguments are: (1) "Vegetarians are bores." Answer: Granted. But if a bore is right? Bores talk about so many things they must be right in some. (2) "The change is inconvenient." Answer: Less so every year, and our personal convenience matters nothing. (3) "Brussels sprouts and puffiness." Answer: Serve them right. The abuse of a diet is no argument against its use. (4) Doctors don't advise it. Answer: Reforms in the matter of the preservation of health have been generally started outside of the medical profession rather than from within. So with other professions. (5) A meat-eating Englishman is a finer man than a rice-eating Oriental. Answer: A most dubious generalization, and quite irrelevant. No one can argue from foreigners to ourselves, the question at once becomes intolerably complex. We have quite enough to do to distinguish cause and effect among ourselves only. (6) You always assume a meat diet is excessive in amount, but there is no evidence of a moderate consumption of animal food being prejudicial in the same way. Answer: We are considering especially full-blooded healthy boys with strong appetites and a long tradition of over-eating in the race. No one can foresee a time when vigorous adolescents will not for the most part exceed in eating. The stimulant of meat causes a reaction which provokes further excess—this I can't explain here—but the more pertinent fact is that vegetable stuffs are far less heating to the blood, and in their case excess does not lead to the same results; that is among our countrymen—never mind anybody else. Of course the inductive evidence is incomplete, but in all urgent matters man must be content with probability, as my physician has said. (7) But a whole lot of sensible high-minded men are against you, and have lived upright, noble lives without this crankiness. Answer: We are not considering the minority of men gifted either with immunity from concupiscence, or with unusual strength of principle, though they, if they could speak freely, could reveal much grievous shackling of the higher life, and clogging of the soul's wings—but the majority who are almost wholly bereft of these safeguards. (8) But if that is so, then the mischief should be remedied by better home-training and not by crazy experiments. Answer: It is not necessary to talk nonsense on any subject, though as Baron Dowse remarked, "You'll admit it's usual." Every right-minded citizen knows that the strength of the temptation to sins of the flesh is prodigious, and the results of infirmity in combating it are ghastly and beyond words heart-rending. Why then prate against a common-sense way of diminishing that temptation, which at present sweeps away the feeble barriers we now and then try to erect? No one supposes this is the only measure necessary, but to oppose it for the sake of "convenience" in deference to a blind prejudice is, in the sight of Heaven, unmitigated lunacy. (9) Yes, but in calling it blind prejudice you are arrogantly assuming the right to dub countless generations of the foremost races of mankind utter fools. Answer: I said "blind"; you can't read that once fashionable book, the Bible, without recognizing that we ought never to expect a large majority of people to be on the side of any truth whatever.

Why should we suppose that in a matter so bound up with sense-pleasure as feeding, the heedless multitude has acted rightly? For notice, it is a question of acting more than judging. Numbers among us secretly approve of clean feeding so long as nobody asks them to adopt it. Anyhow a little reflection on 1 Cor. iii. 19, will cure you of talking about the "foremost" races of men as if their numbers made them wise. (10) O bother your arguments; I don't want to do it, and there's an end of it. Answer: Now you are speaking like an honest man; it would have saved a deal of trouble if you had said this at first.

Well, Henry, you will pardon this jaw. You see in all other matters you have manifested a singular absence of prejudice. Not so in this. Please observe that I have touched on only one side of a big question—the educational. But have you ever thought of the singular fact that on the humanitarian side it looks as if mankind were reluctantly being drawn up to a higher level of thought and feeling; very reluctantly and very partially. I mean that once, about 2000 B.C., the majority of thinking people never doubted that the sacrifice of the first-born was a duty. The next stage they passed to was to substitute animals for their sacrifices. Possibly the eating of flesh came in or was instigated by this practice, but why should it be thought incredible that our practice of killing animals for the mere pleasure of eating them is a stage in development from which we are summoned to rise? Anyhow, once grant that there is evidence that we can subsist in good health without flesh of beasts—and nobody doubts it—it cannot be right to go on slaughtering them by the million for food. And if it is not right it is very very wrong; a huge collective *injuria* for which all are partly responsible except those who are literally forced to conform to a vicious custom because it is prevalent. If this reasoning is anywhere near being true, ought we not to connect the crime with the calamities which have supervened?

Be all this as it may be, think, if this grave aspect of the matter presents itself to a horny old bachelor like me, how much more definitely to you as a bringer-up of your own sons! Now, having galled the tenderest sore place in a Briton's constitution, I must

stop. What a blessing to be writing to a man whose bristles
never stand permanently on end!

Yours,

J.

P.S.—I have just heard an interesting fact which ought to
be widely known. You notice that in writing on vegetarianism
I omitted a lot of physiological arguments in its favour, not
wanting to be prolix, e.g. its effects on low spirits, sea-sickness,
demand for long sleep, etc., and also because these are matters of
individual concern. But what do you make of this when we are
confronted with the tremendous "Colour Problem"? From
more than one well-informed authority I learn that of all
barriers between us and the Chinese, there is none so insur-
mountable as the hideous fact that all meat-eating people offend
their sense of smell! Imagine what it would be if it were the
other way round, that owing to a foul diet the reason for which
cannot be explained, we found a whole nation noisome to our
senses; how we should think it a mark of our high breeding
and natural superiority to spurn them as so much rubbish! I
prophesy the day will come when to our descendants, just as the
spirit of religious persecution has become to us unthinkable, so
the state of barbarism denoted by flesh-eating, slaughter-houses,
butcher's shops, etc., will be an unimaginable horror.

Don't fling this letter on to your dust heap till you get the
next. It will be short and, I think, inoffensive.

Yours ever,

JAMES.

Letter XCVI

Dear Henry:

For some time after I first had qualms about mutton-
chops, the fact which chiefly gave me pause was that some of
the best men I know were solidly against the change of diet
which I was contemplating. Not because they were in good case
without it, but for some far worthier reason.

Well, I found it was as follows: they regarded the whole
subject as insignificant, and that to give thought to it was to

become a prey to a needless meticulosity, especially when our minds ought in these days to be occupied with the weightier matters of the law, justice, mercy, etc. Suppose a citizen gave his energies to denouncing the wearing of hats on the ground that baldness was increased thereby. He would be undoubtedly right, but a noodle all the same: for we are not in this world to rate baldness as the most urgent evil. "So," say they, "is your fruitarian. When society is reeling with intestine strife and the infant League of Nations is slowly learning to walk, we had better leave food questions alone as unimportant: practise moderation, of course, but don't go about the globe telling people they will be judged according as they eat ham or tomatoes. For the less you think about food the better."

Good sense, no doubt: but it is our business to distinguish one thing from another. The most showy hat is an external: food affects the inside; and even granting the weight of the argument about baldness, there is a sinister allusion in Holy Writ to a "hairy scalp" which you might look up. The contention suffers from the slight drawback of being untrue. No question that touches on the purity of heart of your own son is a trifle: and a professing Christian who has persuaded himself that it is, is worse than a bore or a crank: he is a madman. I admit it is no joke to suppose that our forefathers were mainly wrong: but who can look round on the world to-day and suppose that they were wholly wise? And if they were wrong in anything why not in this?

But, dear friend, don't bother to write about so painful a topic; as, of course, it will distress you. I should have "let sleeping dogs lie" if you had not mooted the question the other day. My difficulty then was that these particular dogs are not sleeping, though as far as I can judge they are lying!

Yours,

JAMES.

Letter XCVII

Dear James,

I went down the other day to see Jack at his preparatory school, kept by a Mr ——, and had some interesting talk with the latter, whom I found exercised about the purity question. He says the well-to-do mothers on this subject are unspeakable:

they nearly all intimate gently but firmly that growing boys require plenty of good food; you know the formula; and how that if he were to take a sensible line on this matter, i.e. constraining the youngsters to chew their food and stop eating when they had had enough, he would soon be a ruined man. Did you ever? But he went on to explain that the mischief shows itself later, that is during the public school age, and to prepare his boys for that trial he made a practice of giving them careful instruction on the laws of nature, as they left his school for the larger world, adding, "Of course it is the parents' job, but they won't do it, except a few, so I have to."

I came away rather uneasy, not knowing what to do, but seeing that it is a task which requires expert handling if the venture is not to do harm. Have you any ideas? I don't think you have given me anything yet, nor is it quite plain how the thing is to be fitted to the main principle you have insisted on.

Yours ever,

H.

Letter XCVIII

My dear Henry,

You remember our agreeing on the starting-point of this problem, viz. that children born self-gratifying by instinct, unless checked, will grow up so, but that their self-gratification will take various forms. How vast is the realm of tomfoolery, to be sure! Having allowed their sons to grow up hedonists, people cannot understand that it will depend on the temperament whether sensuality gains the upper hand or pride. Nobody can possibly foresee which; the only thing quite certain is that it will be one or the other or both.

It came to my knowledge—I forget how—that some of our schoolmasters were giving close attention to the subject, and there was some printed matter worth reading. I soon came to the conclusion that the practical issues were extremely simple, if only the common-sense rules were observed. But it is always extremely easy to do the right thing in the wrong way, and to implant a worse lie in a boy's mind than any that are there already.

To begin with, any instruction given by an adult, no matter how wisely, how tactfully, how sympathetically, if it is not based on the child's reverence for God, will inevitably induce him to believe that he can save himself from selfishness by prudence—the primeval lie, more rampant to-day than ever.

The object of the instruction—which ought to be given partially by the mother at about nine years of age—is that the child shall connect *all* problems, both physical and spiritual, with his Maker. Nothing else matters much compared with this. We are not training the boy simply to be chaste, but to reverence his body as God's handiwork, and because he is entrusted with the wondrous gift of procreation. If this teaching is given simply and reverently, very little *warning* is needed. Of all subjects it is the best for linking together conduct and religion, the divine and the human, self-knowledge with the knowledge of God.

Of course people, fathers especially, are shy and awkward and desperately timid. But there is no excuse for shirking this plain duty. They have only to write—so I am informed—to the White Cross League, Dean's Yard, Westminster, and ask for the papers for schoolboys, and they will find a leaflet giving exactly the teaching required; this they can give to their sons one by one, *to be read in their presence,* just before public school life begins. After the reading, which had better be twice, the father has only to extract a promise that if any trouble of any kind comes at school, the boy will let him know. I should add that there are two leaflets, one more explicit than the other, to suit different tastes. The best of this plan is that it saves the father from the real difficulty which is to find the right mean between outspokenness and wrong suggestion.

I gather that some schoolmasters are doing good work, but it is patently a task belonging to the father and mother; the latter's place is—but it is all explained in the leaflets.

Yours ever,

J.

Letter XCIX

My dear James,

I thought I had finished worrying you with my practical problems, but here's another. The boys are badgering me to let them go ever so often to the cinema which has been opened in ——, two miles away, no motor, stuffy atmosphere, dubious company. In short, nothing will induce me to give leave. But I have been led to reflect on the prevalence of these "shows" and to harbour misgivings about their effect on the swarms of children who attend them for three hours on end, night after night. Moreover the preparatory schoolmaster who has charge now of my offspring inveighs against the shows on various grounds, and I think he must be disinterested because if he carted a big bevy of his brats to the show for an entire evening, perhaps he would be free of his burden and able to "possess his soul" for a bit, which is rapidly becoming a lost art. How in the world can a man teach for thirteen weeks on end if his mind is without nourishment all the time?

Yours ever,

H.

Letter C

My dear Henry,

A prevalent opinion appears to be that the cinema shows, with unrestricted attendance of children, make no particular difference to education. Something—not very much perhaps—has been done to banish undesirable films from the shows, and it is supposed that many a cottage mother is thankful to be quit of her offspring for two or three hours every evening and to feel a vague assurance that they are taking no harm. This easy-going view is contradicted by fact. For young people the shows are pernicious, yet they might easily be made beneficial.

What is the chief obstacle to good teaching in our elementary schools? Simply the size of classes, which makes it utterly impossible for the teacher to train the reasoning faculty. We love to hoodwink ourselves with a wholly fictitious view of what is happening. A large proportion of the so-called educated classes are loud in asserting that our industrial disputes would speedily be ended if the working men could be got to understand elementary political economy. Others affirm, with much evidence in their favour, that the power of reasoning—as distinct from that of talking—is almost as conspicuous by its absence from the well-to-do classes as from the multitude. Whichever view be adopted there is a consensus that failure, huge and apparently irremediable, dogs the footsteps of our trainers of children's *minds.* We are not concerned for the moment with physical or ethical training, but with the intellectual; and everybody knows that when tested by the only fair test, that is by the proportion of students who leave the schools eager to go on learning simply from interest in the subject, all class-teaching of boys in what is called book work and to a less degree of girls also, fails. There is a disposition among the boys to work if they can be got to see that their livelihood depends upon it. But that has nothing to do with intellectual interest, and it was Herbart, I think, who remarked that any motive for intellectual effort, except interest in the subject, is bad for the character. (There need be no dispute about the abuse of this theory of interest. Let us anyhow agree that the thing to aim at is that effort could be made by the pupils *in the hope of discovery*; nothing to do with "spoon feeding.")

Now any honest estimate of this training given in our schools is bound to be depressing. The number of boys who after school-life pursue learning for its own sake is surprisingly small; and even of them the majority go off into subjects which they have not been taught in class, rather than into the school subjects. Optimists of course allege that the mental capacity subsequently revealed by some is due to the class teaching. I doubt it, but will not dispute the matter here. The indisputable is enough to make any teacher groan, viz. that very few young people are stirred to exert themselves as if there were truth ahead of them to enter into and enjoy; and this beggarly result is the outcome of the best efforts made by our most competent teachers under the most favourable conditions, that is, in classes numbering—in the big public schools—not more, if possible, than twenty-five. The idea is that the double aim of class-teaching is best secured by some such compromise between the quiet penetrating appeal of a *tête-à-tête* talk, and the stimulus given by a group; by rivalry and the spur of publicity. But any teacher of English schoolboys from fourteen to seventeen, unless he be preternaturally callous, must know that as soon as he appeals to the reasoning faculties and demands an effort of reflection a considerable proportion of his hearers fail to follow him; his language becomes strange to them, though but now it was easy to understand. In other words, as long as he was telling them bare facts he might be dull, but he was intelligible; the moment he requires the linking of facts by apprehension of their relations, no matter how sparkling his talk may be, he only carries a few of his hearers with him[1].

Another baffling consideration is that the larger the audience the slower is the general apprehension, in proportion as the emotions are more excitable[2].

Since then, in class teaching the aim is only rarely to touch the emotions, but rather to implant new ideas, it is obvious that the larger the class the greater the failure.

Such are some of the obstacles against which our patient teachers have to contend. Many abandon all hope of teaching their pupils to think; but the more alert are casting about for subjects less "bookish"; more of the nature of handicraft or, better, choral-singing, so as to ensure anyhow an activity on the part of all in place of the listening which is virtually inertia.

Now such being the problem, what is the influence of the cinema?

Clearly everything depends on how it is used. A picture vivifies the spoken word and deepens the impression provided that it deals with the same subject. If it does not, it is merely wearisome or worse, distracting. The cinemas as at present used are both, especially the latter; for the pictures shown have probably no connexion whatever with the school lessons, but there is enough excitement about them to secure a transient attention, the effect of which must be to obliterate the faint memory of the lessons, and by hurrying the mind from one impression to another to induce the worst kind of smattering, that which depends on pleasurable sensation, not on thought; and which is pleasurable because it involves no effort of thinking and only the minimum of attention.

---

[1] This is not only because no two brains work at the same speed, but because one mind uses a process of inference and conclusion which appears to be different from that of others. An expert in the training of "dunces" has declared that what a schoolmaster calls a dunce is simply a boy who pursues truth by a road which the master has never trodden, and that it would be more accurate to describe the dunces as the original minded, and the quick prize-winners as the stupid, or anyhow, commonplace.

[2] The great preacher, St Francis de Sales, used to say that if he wished to implant a new idea and not merely stir the feelings, he preferred a small congregation to a large one. So Christ gave most of His attention to training the chosen few rather than to moving multitudes.

One effect, of course, must be to make all other sorts of teaching seem dull in comparison. That is to say, the regular teachers are heavily handicapped, not only by the hopeless size of the classes, but because the children come to them already the victims of two delusions:

(1) That the lesson is likely to be a bore.

(2) That there is a way of learning far more rapidly and without exertion. That is to say, a grievous infirmity of the English mind is encouraged, and the crushing burden laid upon the devoted men and women who are labouring to lift the thoughts of the children and show them the joy of discovering truth, is made more crushing still.

It is advisable to remind ourselves that what we are in search of is a method not of keeping children out of mischief or of plastering their minds with scraps of any information they can be induced to listen to, but with giving them new and true ideas about life. Ideas are not made to grow in helter-skelter fashion and at random; but by a sequence from the known to the unknown; by the deepening of impressions made by facts presented by the senses; by a combining of the self-evident. But the serious indictment brought against the uncontrolled attendance by children at the cinema is that the presentation of facts is far too rapid, and there is no coherent sequence. Nothing is learnt, but the sensations are tickled, and the result is plainly to be traced in widespread superficiality of mind and restless craving for the stimulus of sensationalism.

I well remember an instructive incident in a railway carriage some thirty years ago. Scene: an artizan and wife and a very fidgety boy of about two years, and opposite me in the far corner an old lady in widow's weeds, reading, strangely enough, a good book. Thinking I knew something about children, I suggested to the parents that they should show the child pictures to keep him quiet. The old lady interposed: "Sir, I fear you don't know much about children." I admitted I was a lorn bachelor, but ready to learn. She then told me she had recently lost a very promising grand-child whose parents often used to show him pictures, exciting his brain by a very severe demand till he died of meningitis. "A quick child exerts every faculty to the utmost to find a meaning to a picture, just as any scholar knows there is no mental effort so severe as making out a half-obliterated inscription on a stone. Of course if the pictures change quickly the effect is worse still." I had nothing to say.

The pity is that all this mischief, deplorable though it is, is a bagatelle compared with the moral effect of the cinema. I am not going to hammer in the familiar warning against encouragement of crime, because we are fairly awake when our pockets are threatened; nor am I going to accuse County Councils of allowing obscene films; but I give the reluctant testimony of a town clergyman who spoke with knowledge: "The effect of four years of the cinema in this town is that the children take interest in sexual matters a year earlier than they did."

If there is any genuineness in the oft repeated demand that our education must be improved, these heinous abuses will be ruthlessly stamped out. It could be done by the simple provision that no child under sixteen be allowed to attend an ordinary show; but that, wherever possible, carefully selected pictures *connected with their lessons in school*, should be shown to an audience of children, once or twice a week, slowly, with pauses between, and explained by someone who knows the subject and can talk English distinctly.

Unless efforts are speedily made in this direction we shall deserve all the evil that must befall us. But we shall not relish it. It will be what Tom Hood called "little joy."

Yours ever,
JAMES.

Letter CI

My dear James,

It is a strange but very common way of showing gratitude to demand a further favour, and yet I cannot think that you will take it amiss if that is what I venture to do. I don't suppose you want to be thanked in the ordinary way, so if you would look on this letter as a sort of expression of gratitude for really precious benefits, I should be glad.

What I want still is not so much guidance in obscurity, as an answer to the question which has been before us all along. Can we say now what education is? I seem to have learnt enough to give me a new hope in my own task—aye and in my own life too—but still to be quite at sea as to forecasting the future, or as to advising any friend about his son's profession. Can it be that our best rules only apply to the present, while our perplexities are concerned with the future?

Yours ever,

HENRY.

Letter CII

My dear Henry,

I will do what I can, but if anyone should say he could put a fairly adequate statement of what the training up of an immortal child really is into a letter, I should be quite sure of one thing—he has not learnt the ABC of the matter yet.

One thing it certainly is not. It is not a constraining or compelling or persuading of a young human being to behave or even to be as the parents would *naturally* like him to, that is, in conformity to unreflecting worldly opinion; because the more complete the conformity, the more stunted the individuality. That, if agreed to, carries us far for a negative. I mean that the mischief of such a training is inherent in the most pious-sounding programme ever devised, unless we see its limitations. Suppose we understand so much—a vast deal more than many good folk have ever dreamt, viz. that it is the implanting of principle that tells, not the insisting on respectable conduct; it still remains a deadly danger that the truest principles may be turned into swine-husks unless they ferment in the heart as something *living*. So far the New Testament guides us very distinctly. Now what next? how are the principles to be made to ferment?

To this question the most manifold answers are given, most of them crazily assuming that you have only got to tell a child the truth and he will learn it; whereas it is clear that man can only "plant" and "water," but that "God gives the increase." Also that the planting and watering are difficult enough because they include environment, not only talk, but the imparting of the life itself is God's gift; always a miracle, supremely marvellous to anyone who receives it, and yet—such is the condescension of the Most High—dependent on man's playing his part here also. What part?

Now we are brought up against the very crux of the problem of life. The vast majority of us want to do what is right, but we don't like having to own that we have no health in us, only a power to receive; and that that power itself depends on our *desiring* the thing which is offered—God's Righteousness—far more intently than anything else whatever, even what we call the happiness of those whom we love, or the visible evidence of our success in working the work of God on earth.

The upshot of which is that the only true educator is the parent, who is in a constant state of thankfulness, as he is in constant contact with Christ, and among all his activities, schemes and hopes, prays incessantly and hopefully that God will "give the increase" in the bringing up of his child; perfectly content to leave *every* result in His hands; never worrying, but never ceasing to ask, and to yearn.

What then is education? Some knowing people cling to an absurd derivation of the word, following Socrates in thinking that whatever we learn are ideas which have been really in the mind from the beginning, and that education means a "drawing out." There is not much in my opinion to be said for the theory, but nothing at all for the derivation: if it meant "drawing out" the word would be "eduction"; and a modern scholar decides in favour of the meaning of "feeding" rather than that of "training" (as one trains vine shoots, etc.). Let us then apply the idea of feeding to the matter in hand.

We need not be surprised if light is shed for us from the Lord's Prayer. Observe, the fourth petition is a reminder that we are in a state of sin still, for if we were perfect we should be wholly sustained by the perfect holiness[1]; but like Gen. iii. it is also an announcement of salvation (John vi. 33 *sqq.*) because every meal ought to be a Eucharist; every horror in life a stepping stone to something higher; even the sinful state itself is a stage in the manifesting of God's glory. Now if this be true—and if it is not there is no God—the "feeding" of a child is a dealing rightly with him as sinful, so that he may learn to co-operate with God in turning that sinfulness into a permanent state of blessedness by being transformed.

This fact he has to learn is so unspeakably sublime that one

[1] Cf. *The Lord's Prayer*, by R. M. Benson, a very precious little volume.

would think that merely as knowledge it would be the "food from Heaven," but it is more, it is Life itself; and Jack being "educated" is being fed with natural food for the mind which is gradually transformed into spiritual food, every knock being turned into a blessing, every innocent joy into a foretaste of Heaven. He will not understand this yet awhile; but mark this, O Henry, I beg you mark it: *his understanding it some day depends on your understanding it now.*

A week ago I foolishly supposed I might define education for you. Why, bless me! though I have tried to state it broadly, I have hardly touched the fringe of the subject! What a task is before you! and how blest are you in knowing that to it you are plainly called!

Macte esto, frater dilectissime.

Your aff.

J.

For EU product safety concerns, contact us at Calle de José Abascal, 56–1°,
28003 Madrid, Spain or eugpsr@cambridge.org.

 www.ingramcontent.com/pod-product-compliance
Ingram Content Group UK Ltd.
Pitfield, Milton Keynes, MK11 3LW, UK
UKHW012334130625
459647UK00009B/284